The Tuskegee Syphilis Study

THE TUSKEGEE SYPHILIS STUDY

THE REAL STORY AND BEYOND

FRED D. GRAY

Black Belt Press

Montgomery

The Black Belt Press

P.O. Box 551

Montgomery, AL 36101

Design by Randall Williams
Printed in the United States of America
03 02 01 00 99   5 4 3 2 1

The Black Belt, defined by its dark, rich soil, stretches across central Alabama. It was the heart of the cotton belt. It was and is a place of great beauty, of extreme wealth and grinding poverty, of pain and joy. Here we take our stand, listening to the past, looking to the future.

To my wife,
BERNICE
(1934–1997)
Without her encouragement and assistance,
I would never have written this book.

To the seven living survivors of the Tuskegee Syphilis Study,
CHARLES POLLARD
HERMAN SHAW
CARTER HOWARD
FRED SIMMONS
ERNEST HENDON
GEORGE KEY
FREDERICK MOSS.

And to the memory of the
616 DECEASED PARTICIPANTS OF THE STUDY.

Listing of Study Participants, 1932–1972

Adair, Green
Adams, Courtney
Adams, James
Adams, Louis
Albert, Prince
Alexander, Ben
Alexander, Joe
Alexander, Marion
Allen, Jefferson
Allen, Sam
Allen, Selden
Anderson, George
Anderson, George T.
Anthony, Will
Askew, Sebon
Austin, Alfred
Austin, Dean
Austin, George
Austin, Hyth
Austin, Nelson
Austin, Wiley
Baker, George
Banks, Early
Banks, Jack
Barrow, David
Barrow, Seth
Battle, Enoch
Battle, Lee
Beasley, Robert
Beasley, Nathaniel
Berry, John
Berry, Leornie
Bessick, Edward
Bessick, Ernest
Black, Ishman
Black, Jim
Black, Tommie Lee
Black, Wiley
Blackburn, Will
Blackman, Prismus
Bledsoe, Pustell

Borum, Muncie
Boyd, Grant
Boyd, Jimmie
Boyd, Richard
Boyd, Tobe
Brooks, Ealy (Eli)
Brown, Bailey, Jr.
Brown, Doll
Brown, John C.
Brown, K. L.
Brown, Logan
Brown, Riley
Brown, Vance
Bryant, J. R.
Bryant, Willie
Bryant, Winfield
Buchanan, Ben
Buchanan, Charlie
Buchanan, Columbus
Buchanan, Gene
Buchanan, John
Buchanan, Sol
Buchanan, Wash
Buford, James
  (Clemmie)
Burton, William
Buscom (Bascomb),
  Bishop
Butler, Eli
Byrd, Sam
Caldwell, William
Calhoun, Forney
Campbell, Alfred
Campbell, Charlie
Campbell, Ishmael
Campbell, Jack
Campbell, Judge
Campbell, Will
Carlisle, Robert
Carmichael, Gus
Carr, Jim

Caston Eugene
Caupbell, Charlie
Chambless, William
Chambliss, Henry
Chambliss, Jerry
Chambliss, Pollard
Chappel, Seaborn
Chappell, Hilliard
Charleston, Rufus
Chatman, Georgie
Cheeks, John
Chisholm, Ben
Chisholm, Ed
Clabon, James
Clark, Joshua
Clark, Moses
Clements, Ludie
Cole, Allen
Coleman, Samuel
Collier, Isaac
Collins, Algie
Collins, Jim
Collins, John
Collins, Julius
Collins, Relice
Collins, Willie
Collis, Dan
Collis, Sylvester
Comer, Ben
Cooper, Amos
Cooper, Frank
Cooper, Gentry
Cox, Fletcher
Cox, Jeff
Cox, Redonia
Cox, Tom
Crawford, George
Crawford, Jimmie
  Lee
Crawford, John
Crawford, Logan

Crawford, Wash
Crawley, James
Crayton, Ernest
Crayton, Lonzo
Daniel, Albert
Daniel, Clark
Daniel, John Wesley
Daniel, Mac
Darkey, Floyd
Davis, Anthony
Davis, Bonnie
Davis, Elbert
Davis, Henry
Davis, Meriman
Davis, Martin
Day, Frank
Demps, Benjamin
Dennis, Nat
Dixon, Frank
Doggett, Zettie
Donar, Sam
Donar, Kelley
Donar, Mose
Doner, Wilbert
Doner, Wiley
Dorsey, Aleck
Dorsey, Jim
Dorsey, Will
Dowdell Crawford
Downer, Willie
Dozier, Bill
Driscoll, Harvey
Dubose, N. D.
Echols, D. C.
Echols, John
Echols, Presley
Echols, Wade
Echols, Wiley
Echols, Willie
Ellington, John A.
Ellington, Samuel

Epps, Henry
Evans, Ben
Evans, Henry Mark
Evans, Lemuel
Felton, Cleve
Felton, Tom
Fitzpatrick, Green
Fitzpatrick, Ned
Fitzpatrick, Tom
Fitzpatrick, Willie
Foote, Bill
Foote, Joe
Ford, Abbie
Ford, Arthur
Ford, Percy
Fort, Calvin
Fort, E. Gary
Fort, Jasper
Fort, Nathan
Fort, Sandy
Foster, Archie
Foster, Ben Eddie
Foster, Bonnie
Foster, David
Foster, Lee
Foster, Pomp
Foster, Reuben
Foster, William
Foy, Jim
Foy, Louis
Franklin, Ulysses
Gaines, Percy
Galgher, Ben
Gamble, Bob
Gamble, Elijah
Garner, Alfred
Gaston, Will
Gauchett, Nick
Germany, Albert
Germany, Fred
Gholston, Ben
Giles, Fred
Gilmer, Quince
Gilmore, Doc

Glenn, Sam
Goode, John
Goodson, G. C.
Gordon. Virgil
Gray, Desibe
Greathouse, Clabon
Greathouse, Clifton
Greathouse, John E.
Green, Mose
Green, Walter
Green, Will
Greer, George
Griffin, Colonel
Griffin, Dave
Griffin, Samuel
Griggs, Charlie
Grimes, Emmett
Grimes, James
Grove, Frank
Hagins, G. B.
Hagood, Andrew
Hall, Cary
Hamilton, Columbus
Haney, Sherman
Hann, Freeman
Hardy, Albert
Harper, Clifton
Harper, Robert
Harris, Adolphus
Harris, Alonzo
Harris, Elisha
Harris, George
Harris, Jak
Harris, Jake
Harris, James
Harris, Louis
Harris, Theodore
Harris, Will
Harris, Will
Harris, William
Harrison, Edward
Harrison, Willie, Sr.
Hart, Frank
Hart, John

Hart, L. Z.
Harvey, Charlie
Harvey, Walter
Hatten, Ludie
Hatten, Sandy
Hatton, Square
Hawkins, Henry
Henderson, Absolomi
Henderson, Hilliard
Henderson, James
Henderson, Wilbur
(Dick)
Hendon, Ernest
Hendon, Louie
Henry, Johnnie
Hicks, Phil
Hicks, William
Hill, Phillip
Hoffman, Clayborn
Holliday, Joseph
Holmes, Zan
Howard, Carter
Howard, Tony
Hudson, John
Huffman, Benny Lee
Huffman, Marcus
Hughly, Arthur
Hurt, Will
Hutchinson, Zack
Iszell, Minor
Jackson, David
Jackson, Fleming
Jackson, Isiah
Jackson, James
Jackson, Martin
Jackson, Randall
Jackson, Roosevelt
Jackson, Stephie
Jackson, Tom
Jackson, Tommy J.
Jackson, Jim
James, Clifton
James, John C.
James, George

James, Jessie
James, Wilbert
Jenkins, Howard
Jenkins, West
Jenkins, Wiilliam, Jr.
Jenkins, Willie
Jernigen, Will
Johnson, Price
Johnson, Charles
Johnson, Faegin
Johnson, G. C.
Johnson, Jimmie
Johnson, Johnnie J.
Johnson, Simon
Johnson, Spencer
Johnson, Sylvester
Johnson, Thomas
Johnson, Thomas
J.C.
Jonakings (Jernigan),
Jim
Jones Chancy
Jones, Clifford
Jones Dan Jeff
Jones, Hayes
Jones, Henry
Jones, Major
Jones, Roosevelt
Jones, Shepherd L.
Jones, Willie
Jones, Willie Moffett
Jorden, James
Julkes, Albert
Julkes, Ephrom
Julkes, Warren
Kelly, Ad Kelly
Kelly, John K.
Kelly, Mitchell
Kennebrew, Usher
Key, Charlie B.
Key, George
Key, Henry
Key, Jesse
Key, Ned

Key, Nathan
Kindell, R. T.
Kitt, Edmond
Laine, Nathaniel
Lane, John Edward
Lane, Johnnie W.
Lane, Wylie
Laster, James
Laury, Andrew
Levett, William
Lewis, Peter M
Lewis, Sherman
Ligon, Riley
Lockett, George
Lockwood, W. P.
Long, Sim
Long, Will
Love, Milton
Loveless, Ed
Loyd, Ernest
Macon, V. M.
Maddox, Jesse
Mahone, Dave L.
Mahone, Fonzie
Manley, Charlie Y.
Martin, Governor
Martin, Lewis
Martin, Roosevelt
Martin, Wesley
Mason, Frazier
Mays, Clabon
McGrady, Thomas
McKee, Essex
McMullen, Wash
McNeill, Willie
Menefee, Joe
Menefee, John
Miles, William
Mims, Richard
Mindingall, Samuel
Mitchell, Gary
Mitchell, John
Moore, Aaron
Moore, Abner

Moore, Alonzo
Moore, Ezekial
Moore, Felix
Moore, Frank
Moore, Marshall
Moore, Willie Bill
Morgan, Lenza
Morris, Hobbie
Moss, Frank
Moss, Frederick
Moss, Grant
Moss, John J.
Moss, Otis
Motley, Peter
Mott, Julius
Murphy, Dock
Murray, Albert
Mutry, Jim
Myrick, I. S.
Neal, Rubin
Neal, Rufus
Norwood, Ed
Nunley, Willie
O'Neal, Thaddaus
Ogletree, York
Pace, Eddie
Pace, Elmore
Pace, Evans
Pace, George
Pace, Henry
Pace, Lonzie
Pace, Nelse
Pace, Steve
Pace, Otis
Padgett, Whitelaw
Parker, Eli
Patrick, Will
Patterson, Cleveland
Paulk, Frank
Payne, Ludie
Pearsall, Pender
Pearson, Ed
Pendleton, John
Philips., Tom

Phillips Charlie
Phillips, Ed
Phillips, John W.
Phillips, Ned
Phillips, Prince
Philpot, Roland
Pinkard, Charlie
Pinkard, Charles Lee
Plezes, Walter
Polk, Albert
Pollard, Charlie
Pollard, Elbert
Pollard, Lucius
Pollard, Osburn
Pollard, Vertis
Pollard, Will
Pollard, Woody
Porch, Bertha
Potts, Jethro
Pruitt, Taylor
Pugh, Armistead
Pugh, Arthur
Randolph, Joe
Randolph, Johnnie
Randolph., Major
Randolph, Robert
Ray, George
Ray, William
Reed, Andrew
Reed, Douglas
Reed, Fletcher
Reynolds, Charles
Reynolds, Gus
Rhone, C. H.
Ries, Clinton
Robbins, Tom
Roberson, Lige
Robert, Bob Lee
Robinson, Albert
Robinson, Butler
Rockamore, Ben
Rogers, Henry
Rowell, Charlie
Rowell, Edmond

Rowell, Theodore
Ruff, R. L.
Rush, Lieutenant
Rush, Wash
Russell, Clarence
Russell, Jeff
Russell, Willie McK.
Samuel, Bill
Samuel, George
Samuel, Odell
Samuel, Tom George
Sanford, E.
Sanford, Fletcher
Scott, Lester
Scott, 0. T.
Scott, William
Seatts, John
Shaw, Charlie
Shaw, Herman
Shelton, John
Shelton, Purvis
Shumpert, Paul
Simmons, Fred
Simmons, John
Simpson, Bennie
Simpson, Jimmie
Sinclair, Anderson, Jr.
Sinclair, Oscar
Sistrunk, Henry
Slaughter, John
Smith, Cain
Smith, Dudley
Smith, Eugene
Smith, Hilliard
Smith, Jimmie
Smith, Joe
Smith, John Wesley
Smith, Lieutant
Smith, Low
Smith, Richard
Smith, Robert
Harvey
Smith, Thomas K.
Sparks, Ed

Speed, Olin
Spivey, Jim
Stewart, Mack
Story, Millard
Swanson, Mark
Swanson, Please
Swanson, Tom
Swanson, Tump
Swanson, Will B.
Swanson, Willie
Swift, Lawrence
Swift, Son
Swint Andrew
Talbert, Oscar
Talley, Louis
Tarver, Eugene
Tarver, Oscar
Tate, Edward
Tate, Louis
Tate, Robert Lee
Tatum, Mayso
Taylor, Richard
Tatum, Sylvester
Taylor, Van
Taylor, Warren
Temple, George
Theney, Bob
Thomas, Jessie
Thomas, Oran

Thomas, Pat
Thompson, Pete
Thompson, Willie
Tinsley, Edison
Todd, Walter
Tolbert, George
   Washington
Tolbert, Jim
Tolbert, Ocie
Tramble, Willie
Trammell, Percy
Tredwell, Alf
Turk, Will
Turner, Joe
Turner, West
Turpin, Jim
Tyner, Stephen
Tyson, Freddie, Sr.
Upshaw, Milton
Veal, Coleman
Veal, Jim
Wade, Mitchell
Waggoner, John
Walker, Andrew
Walls, Joe Nathan
Walker, Johnnie W.
Ware, Alex
Warren, Atlee
Warren, Ed

Warren, Sonnie
Watson, John H.
Watson, John L.
Watt, Willie
Weathers, Alonza
Weatherspoon, Sam
Webb, William
Welch, Dan
West, Anthony
Wheat, Tobe
Wheeler, Jake
White, Archie
White, Leonard
White, Sonny
Whitlow, Ed
Whitlow, Motelle
Williams, Albert
Williams, Andrew
Williams, Bill
Williams, Bill Henry
Williams, Bill Jesse
Williams, Coleman
Williams, Eugene
Williams, George
Williams, Henry
Williams, James
Williams, Lewis
Williams, Mathew
Williams, Meshack

Williams, Morris
Williams, Reuben
Williams, Steve J.
Williams, Tom
Willis, J. W.
Willis, Wilbur
Wilson, Govenor
Wilson, Ray
Wilson, Houston
Wilson, Logan
Wimbush, James
Wood, Charlie, Jr.
Wood, Charlie, Sr.
Wood, Louis
Wood, Grant
Woodall, R. D.
Woodall, Nelson
Woolfolk, Jesse
Wright, Jim
Wright, Clarence
Wright, Ernest
Wright, Ludie
Wright, Rev. T. W.
Wright, Will
Wyatt, Tom
Yancey, Booker
Yarbough, Mark
York, Harrison
Young, Jack

Contents

Foreword

When President Clinton, in a ceremony at the White House on May 16, 1997, addressed five elderly African American men—ages 89 to 109—and the family members of others who could not be present, he brought a symbolic resolution to one of the most shameful episodes in U.S. medical history.

The President of the United States looked these men in the eyes and said:

> The United States government did something that was wrong— deeply, profoundly, morally wrong. It was an outrage to our commitment to integrity and equality for all our citizens. . . . The American people are sorry—for the loss, for the years of hurt. You did nothing wrong, but you were grievously wronged. I apologize and I am sorry that this apology has been so long in coming.

As attorney for the participants in what became known as the Tuskegee Syphilis Study, I was deeply moved. Yes, in one sense it was true what the critics were saying, that the President's apology was "too little and too late." Yet for these surviving men and family members, and for the conscience of the nation, it could never be too late to make amends for a terrible injustice. When someone hurts you, their telling you that they are sorry for what they did is a healing act. This is no less true when it is your government that has committed the wrong. World history teaches us that governments rarely admit moral culpability for their wrongful actions.

And what had the United States government done that was so wrong? Put in its simplest terms, the government used 623 men as human guinea pigs in a misguided forty-year medical experiment. That in itself would have been bad enough. The moral and ethical injury was compounded by the fact that all of these men were African American, predominantly poor and uneducated, and were deliberately kept in the dark about what was happening to them.

It is pointless to try to weigh one person's suffering against another's, and I am not for a moment equating the Tuskegee Syphilis Study with the horrors committed in the name of "science" by Nazi doctors against Jews at Dachau and other places during World War II, but the principle is the same. The Nuremberg trials against Nazi war criminals resulted in a set of standards under which the civilized world agreed that human beings would not be used as research animals and that doctors would never forget that their first duty is to heal their patients. The Tuskegee Syphilis Study reiterates the necessity for commitment to these ideals.

As an American citizen, it shames me to realize that the Tuskegee Syphilis Study, which began in 1932, continued under the supervision of U.S. government officials and highly trained medical professionals until 1972, more than two decades after the Nuremberg trials.

Thus, as I sat on the front row in the East Room of the White House on a warm May 16, 1997, I felt the President's apology on behalf of the American people was a significant step in the right direction. Observing the ceremony, I reaffirmed my commitment to help ensure that the lessons of the Tuskegee Syphilis Study were widely known and that some lasting good will come out of the tragic situation.

This book tells the inside story, the real story, of the Tuskegee Syphilis Study, the lawsuit that eventually brought some compensation to the Study victims and survivors, and the events culminating in the White House apology. This book also explains the plans to create a prominent memorial and research center in Tuskegee, Alabama, as a permanent legacy of the experiment and of the rich history and culture of the area.

I wrote this book because God placed me in a position to do so. My first book, *Bus Ride To Justice,* told how I became a civil rights lawyer after growing up in segregated Montgomery, Alabama. My hard-working mother and my supportive community encouraged me to get a college education and then go to law school, even though I had to leave my home state to find a law school that would admit Negroes, as we were then called. After graduating from Case Western Reserve Law School, I could have taken a job in Cleveland, Ohio, but I returned to Alabama, determined to "destroy everything segregated I could find." At the age of twenty-three, I became one of only two African American attorneys in Montgomery. One of my first clients was Rosa Parks, who was arrested after she refused to give up her seat to a white man on a segregated city bus. Subsequently, I became the attorney for the Montgomery Bus Boycott and its inspired leader, the Rev. Dr. Martin Luther King, Jr.

I worked with Martin King, Rosa Parks, E. D. Nixon, and other giants of what mushroomed into the Civil Rights Movement. Between 1955 and 1972, I filed dozens of successful lawsuits to desegregate schools, housing, transportation, places of employment, and other areas of public life. In the mid-1960s I moved my residence forty miles up the road to Tuskegee, Alabama, and in 1970 I became one of the first two African Americans elected to the Alabama legislature since Reconstruction.

Meanwhile, I continued a busy practice in both civil rights and more routine legal matters. I was also a full-time minister in the Church of Christ. I was involved in the community and, I believe it is fair to say, was probably the best-known African American attorney in Alabama.

Yet, until the Tuskegee Syphilis Study became public knowledge through news reports in 1972, I was unaware of the experiment that had existed in my community for forty years. As far as the general public was concerned, the study had been kept a total secret. Nevertheless, when one of the men involved in the study approached me, I immediately recognized the seriousness of what had been done. The man rightfully felt, based on what was being reported in the media, that he had been mistreated and he wanted me to sue whoever was responsible. Consequently, I filed the lawsuit and with the help of my colleagues eventually won a settlement on behalf of all the participants in the study.

Over the years, I remained in close contact with many of the surviving participants. I included a chapter on the case in *Bus Ride To Justice,* which was published in 1995. Then, in 1997, the Home Box Office cable television company presented the dramatic film *Miss Evers' Boys,* which was based on the Tuskegee Syphilis Study. Many of the men involved in the study were deeply offended by this movie, which they felt misrepresented them and the facts of the study. In any case, this movie and a stage play of the same name brought the case back into the media spotlight.

Over a period of time, many people, including myself, realized that even though there had been a settlement in the lawsuit on behalf of the study victims, and the study itself had been ended, there were still unresolved issues that should be addressed. Gradually, the idea emerged for a public apology from the federal government to the victims of the study, including surviving participants and the families of those who had died. For several months, my late wife and I worked together on events which led to the Presidential apology.

Now, using case files, personal knowledge, and interviews and statements of numerous people involved in various aspects of the Study, I have compiled a record which I hope will be compelling and useful reading for students, teachers, researchers, and anyone interested in understanding why and how such an episode could have happened. This book has been written in the hope that the past will not be forgotten and that this type of occurrence will never happen again.

It has been said that those who forget the past are condemned to repeat it. I love my country, and I believe that, through the help of God, the long pendulum of history is slowly swinging in the direction of justice and equality. Nonetheless, the history of African Americans has been too painful to repeat, so we had best remember and remember well.

FRED D. GRAY

Tuskegee, Alabama

Acknowledgments

I am going to tell this story from my perspective as the attorney for the men who were participants in the Tuskegee Syphilis Study, and as a veteran civil rights lawyer. However, this story belongs to Charlie Pollard, Herman Shaw, and the other 621 participants and family members I was privileged to represent. The story also belongs to my late wife, Bernice, who was a meaningful source of encouragement during and after the lawsuit and who was instrumental in the conception of the Tuskegee Human and Civil Rights Multicultural Center.

I acknowledge with gratitude my co-counsel of record, my law partner for more than twenty-five years, Solomon S. Seay, Jr. In addition, over the years, the following attorneys in our law firm assisted: Edwin L. Davis (1926-1998), Charles D. Langford, Cleveland Thornton, Billy Carter, Honorable Aubrey Ford, Walter E. McGowan, Stanley F. Gray, Fred D. Gray, Jr., and Ernestine S. Sapp.

I also acknowledge with great appreciation the assistance James H. Jones gave me during the early stages of *Pollard, et al. v. United States of America, et al.* He located the early records of the Tuskegee Syphilis Study in 410 boxes in the National Archives. These records assisted in settling the lawsuit. Mr. Jones is also the author of *Bad Blood*, and has granted permission to quote portions of his book. He is now a Professor of History at the University of Houston, in Houston, Texas. Notice should also be paid to Peter Buxtun, who courageously called this matter to the attention of the public.

I am grateful for the assistance rendered by Jack Greenburg, who at the time we filed the suit was Director/Counsel of the NAACP Legal Defense Fund. He recommended Michael Sovern, then Dean of Columbia University Law School to serve as legal consultant. I am appreciative to Dean Sovern and Harold Edgar, a professor at Columbia University Law School. They rendered valuable assistance in drafting pleadings, briefs, preparation of settlement documents, and generally serving as legal consultants.

I express my thanks to Joanne C. Bibb, my secretary for thirty years, who has had the primary responsibility in recent years of working with me, the participants and heirs of deceased participants, including serving as an escort for Mr. Herman Shaw to attend the presidential apology. She has rendered valuable service in filing, preserving, and coordinating the records in this case, and in assisting with this book.

I am most appreciative to the late Honorable Preston Hornsby, who was Judge of Probate of Macon County at the time the lawsuit was filed. Without Judge Hornsby's assistance in appointing 463 personal representatives of the estates of the deceased participants, many of the heirs of the deceased participants would not have shared in the proceeds of the settlement.

In addition, I thank Thomas Caver, Clerk of the United States District Court for the Middle District of Alabama, for his assistance with the calculations and disbursements of funds to the participants and the heirs of deceased participants.

I am grateful to the following members of our staff who assisted in various capacities: Alberta Magruder, Trudy B. Powell, Annie L. Bailey, Vanessa Gray Taylor, Patsy D. Smith, and Sherrie P. Cook. Patricia Powell transcribed most of the manuscript.

I am deeply appreciative to my editor, Randall Williams, of Black Belt Press. When I was writing *Bus Ride To Justice*, Randall and I realized many of the cases referred to were of sufficient historical significance to deserve books of their own. At that time, we could only give a summary of those cases. Shortly after the apology, we began to discuss and work on this book. He is everything you would want in an editor, a friend, and a publisher. He has tremendous skill, insight, knowledge, experience, and has greatly assisted in guiding me in the production of this work. I will always be thankful to him and to the members of the staff of Black Belt Press.

Thanks also to the following persons who have read, edited, and given valuable assistance: my brothers, Dr. Abdullah H. Ghandhistani, Judge Thomas W. Gray, and Hugh C. Gray; my sister, Pearl Gray Daniels; and my children, Deborah, Vanessa, Fred Jr., and Stanley.

I am appreciative to Charlie Pollard for coming into my office on July 27, 1972. Without Mr. Pollard's request for legal assistance, the story of the Tuskegee Syphilis Study might have been short-lived and justice for the participants might never have been obtained.

I express my gratefulness to Mr. Herman Shaw, who in recent years has served as spokesman for all of the participants, both living and deceased. I am appreciative to the other 621 men who unknowingly risked their lives in order to help their country in a health care program. I am also appreciative to the family members of the men who have helped me over the years. As a result of their participation, I am committed to keeping their story alive, and to preserve their contributions and the contributions of others in the field of human and civil rights through the Tuskegee Human and Civil Rights Multicultural Center. A portion of the proceeds from this book will go to the Center.

I also thank Jewell Handy Gresham Nemiroff, president of the Hansberry-Nemiroff Fund, who called me after the airing of *Miss Evers' Boys* to express her concern over that production. Mrs. Nemiroff has been consistently supportive and helpful.

Finally, thanks to my friends Robert Burton and James Upshaw for listening, reading, and generally encouraging me to complete this book. We discussed it almost daily during lunch.

The Tuskegee Syphilis Study

1

Introduction

In July 1972, while flying from Washington, D.C., home to Montgomery, I was reading the newspaper when my eye was caught by an article about a medical experiment in my adopted hometown of Tuskegee, Alabama. The article, by Associated Press reporter Jean Heller, described how the study was initiated by the United States Public Health Service in 1932 with the intent of collecting data about the effects of untreated syphilis. According to the article, the study used as subjects some six hundred African American males from the rural areas in and around Macon County, of which Tuskegee is the county seat. More than half of the 623 men had syphilis; the others, a control group, did not.

Over the next few days, additional articles and broadcast reports provided more details. These reports floored me for several reasons.

I was shocked to learn that the study had been going on for forty years. I was born and reared in an adjacent county, and I started handling cases in Macon County soon after I passed the Alabama Bar exam and hung out my shingle in 1954. I had opened a law office in Tuskegee in 1958, had been living there since 1965, and had represented the county in the state legislature. Tuskegee is not a big place. In 1972, the population of the county was only twenty-five thousand, and I had probably shaken the hands of half of them. Yet I had never heard of the Tuskegee Syphilis Study. It was astounding to me that such a study could have avoided public discussion for forty years. I later learned that the medical research community was quite familiar with the study, but that certainly was not the case with the general public.

Secondly, the news story, brief as it was, outlined what could only be viewed as an alarming atrocity and yet another example of racial injustices perpetrated by government in segregated Alabama. In this case, not by the state of Alabama, but by the federal government. Syphilis is an equal-opportunity disease. It can be transmitted from black or white genitals just the same, and it equally ravages black or white neural systems, brains, hearts, and other organs. Yet each of the 623 study subjects was an African American male. Furthermore, they were predominantly poor, uneducated, and, in rural Alabama in 1932, would have been extremely unsophisticated about medical treatment in general. As I said, I was shocked, but I was hardly surprised. I had witnessed many areas where African Americans had been treated unjustly. This case was simply especially appalling because it was officially sanctioned by the federal government and involved life or death situations for several hundred United States citizens.

Thirdly, effective treatment was knowingly and systematically withheld from those suffering from a potentially fatal disease. Putting aside the apparent problems with how the participants were selected, one could see the original rationale behind the Study, for when it began in the thirties, there was no effective cure for syphilis. But by the 1940s, penicillin had been discovered and found to be highly effective as a treatment for syphilis. By the end of World War II, penicillin was a readily available and relatively inexpensive cure for syphilis. Yet for another two decades, officials in charge of this study deliberately withheld treatment from the diseased majority of its participants. I thought it was a tragedy that these poor rural men in my county had suffered such an injustice.

On July 27, 1972, Mr. Charlie Pollard, a Macon County farmer, came into my office and asked if I had read about the men who were involved in the tests for "bad blood." He said he was one of the men. He then related that a few days before, he was at a stockyard in Montgomery and a newspaper woman found him and engaged him in a conversation about his involvement in a health program in Tuskegee since back in the thirties. The reporter asked if he knew Eunice Rivers, the nurse who worked with the men in the testing program from the beginning to end. He stated that he did.

Mr. Pollard related to me in detail his involvement. His statement confirmed the news reports I had been reading and watching on television. As a result of our discussion, I agreed to represent Mr. Pollard in a lawsuit against the government and any others we might discover who were legally responsible for operating and maintaining the study. That is how I became involved as the attorney for the plaintiffs in what became known as *Pollard v. United States of America,* a class action lawsuit filed in federal court in Montgomery.

In the following chapters, I will tell the story of the Tuskegee Syphilis Study, beginning with some background about Macon County. This background is necessary to understanding the time period and setting of the study; the origins and methodology of the study itself; and the filing of the lawsuit, its supporting investigation, the judicial settlement that resulted, and the follow-up legal efforts to locate the participants and their heirs in order to pay them their part of the settlement. Then, I will relate some of what has happened to these men and their case in the years since, especially the renewed media attention of recent years, as well as the unprecedented events of May 1997 when the President of the United States met with some of the study survivors at the White House and publicly apologized to them on behalf of the nation. Finally, I will describe the proposal to build a memorial center in Tuskegee as a legacy to the study participants and to those of all races, particularly Native Americans, European Americans, and African Americans, who have contributed to the unique history and culture of Tuskegee and Macon County, Alabama. This legacy includes legislative and regulatory actions to make sure that such a thing as the Tuskegee Syphilis Study cannot happen again.

2

Macon County, Alabama

A person who was not living in Tuskegee and Macon County in 1932 can hardly imagine what life was like at that time and place. It is hard even for me, and I was born in 1930, in Montgomery, the adjacent county southwest of Macon. To begin with, there were vast material differences. That was long before automatic transmissions in automobiles, televisions, and most of the modern conveniences that we take for granted today. Very few people had ever flown in an airplane. No one had ever heard of an interstate highway. In Macon County and similar rural parts of the Deep South in 1932, most people did not have plumbing, electricity, telephones, and cars, all of which are considered necessities of life now. It truly was a different world then.

Beyond the material, there were the differences in society and culture. Of course, when I speak to schoolchildren today, I am always a little startled by the realization that almost two generations have now reached adulthood in Alabama with no personal knowledge of "colored" water fountains, Jim Crow public accommodations, racial restrictions on voting and jury service, and so forth. This is not to say that all racial problems have been solved, but simply to acknowledge that the South of today is light-years from what it was in 1932.

The part of Alabama which extends from east central Alabama, where Macon County is located, on through Montgomery, Lowndes, Wilcox,

Dallas, Sumter, Greene, and Pickens counties to the Mississippi line, is called "the Black Belt." All of these counties have a majority black population, and many people think the Black Belt is called that because of its demographics. The name was actually bestowed by geologists because of the area's rich, dark soil composition. Nevertheless, while the dark soil was exceptionally fertile, its richness was realized largely through the labor of dark Alabamians. Coincidentally, the name of my publisher, Black Belt Press, is also derived from this region of Alabama which is well-known for its distinctive geographic and socio-political characteristics. Because most people outside Alabama associate "black belts" with martial arts, Black Belt Press prints an explanatory statement (see page 4) in every book it publishes. This statement is a good summary of the culture of the place and hints at the societal extremes—"it was and is a place of great beauty, of extreme wealth and grinding poverty, of pain and joy"—which have existed virtually since Alabama became a state in 1819.

As a center of cotton culture, the Black Belt had a high African American population from the time the first European settlers arrived, bringing with them African slaves. Some of the richest land in Macon County had been a part of the Creek Nation until the cessions of 1832. After the removal of the Indians—another tragic episode in American history—planters and slaves poured into the area. This was a result of the Indian Removal Act of 1830, which authorized the President to negotiate with the Indian tribes east of the Mississippi River for the purchase of their land. The Choctaw, Creek, Tuskegee, Eufaula, Coosa, Alabama, Koweta, Kashita, and other Native American tribes and languages had been early occupants of what is now the State of Alabama. Ultimately, many Indians were isolated far from their fertile homelands on barren, barely habitable land in various desolate areas of the western United States.

Prosperity in Macon County did not last, however, because by 1850 the harsh agricultural practices of the time had "farmed out" some of the best cropland. Between the agricultural decline and the upheaval of the Civil War, Macon County actually lost population in the middle third of the nineteenth century. Still, after emancipation, most of the former slaves stayed in the area and continued to till the soil as sharecroppers or tenant farmers or simply as hired laborers for the white landowners. By 1930, Macon County's population was 27,103, of which 22,320 were African American. According to government statistics, the average income in Macon County was only one to two dollars a day. The 1940 census showed that there were 5,205 farm dwelling units in the county, of which 4,500 were in need of major repairs, had no running water, no electricity, and no toilet within the structure.

In other words, conditions were bad in Macon County in 1932. There were only two incorporated towns, Tuskegee and Notasulga. The Great Depression had begun, and it was harder than ever to earn a living.

Racial Conditions in Alabama

Another very important element which must be considered is the racial climate in Alabama from 1932 to 1954. At that time, in Alabama and throughout the South, everything was rigidly segregated based on race. The laws of the State of Alabama required the complete separation of whites and blacks in public accommodations and in almost all other aspects of life. The United States Supreme Court held in the case of *Plessy v. Ferguson (1896)* that the State of Louisiana could segregate passengers by race on trains traveling in that State so long as the facilities were substantially equal. This was the beginning of the doctrine of "separate but equal," though in practice the result was separate but unequal because facilities provided for "coloreds" rarely if ever were the same as those provided for whites. In 1938, the Court extended that doctrine to education in the case of *Gaines v. Canada, ex rel.* We were thus plagued with "separate but equal" until May 17, 1954. On that day, the Supreme Court held in *Brown v. Board of Education* that separate educational facilities were inherently unequal and that the doctrine of "separate but equal" had no place in the field of education. However, when the Study started, segregation was the law of the land.

In addition, during the beginning and extending into the early phase of the Study, African Americans were still being lynched with sickening regularity. The lives of African Americans in Alabama during that period of time were not worth very much. It was during this time also that the infamous *Scottsboro Boys Case* was making headlines in Alabama and across the nation. This is a case in which two white women accused several African Americans of raping them in north Alabama. Ultimately, in a trial which legal experts have considered biased and based on suspect evidence, the accused were convicted and given life sentences. Several died in prison; one, late in life, was granted a pardon. The point is, that given the racial conditions of the day, it was not difficult for the average white person in Alabama to participate in the Study of untreated syphilis on African American men.

Tuskegee Institute

Because of the existence of Tuskegee Institute, led by Booker T. Washington, there were a larger than average number of well-educated, what would now be called middle-class, African Americans living in Tuskegee. Yet most of the African Americans in Macon County were not middle-class professionals. Most were farmers, a few on their own land but usually on land owned by the white minority. This was still a cotton culture, and cotton culture throughout the Deep South was originally based on slavery and then on tenancy and sharecropping. By the time the Tuskegee Syphilis Study began in 1932, Professor George Washington Carver had already made Tuskegee Institute even more famous by his scientific experiments in agriculture, particularly in developing many uses for peanuts and sweet potatoes. As Robert J. Norrell writes in his book, *Reaping the Whirlwind,* about Tuskegee's civil rights history, Carver's work had not yet changed the dominant agricultural model in Macon County:

> The Institute's efforts to improve farming practices apparently benefited black farmers in Macon County only marginally. Charles S. Johnson, the prominent sociologist at Fisk University, surveyed 612 black farm families in the county in the early 1930s and found that little had changed for the better for black farmers since the end of slavery. Indeed, many things had gotten worse: Land ownership had declined relentlessly. More and more black farmers had become sharecroppers, deepening their dependence on white landlords; ninety percent of those surveyed were tenants. They all told him the same thing:

sharecropping allowed almost no room for blacks to improve themselves. "They manage to live on advances," Johnson wrote, "or by borrowing for food and clothing and permitting their crop to be taken in satisfaction of the debt." For the black tenant, there was very little of the independence that Booker Washington had envisioned. "When you working on a white man's place," one man told Johnson, "you have to do what he says, or treat, trade or travel." The tenant system belied the earlier faith in the curative power of education for blacks: Johnson discovered that black men with more than an elementary education were likely to quit farming altogether. The most successful tenant farmers were those with a bare minimum of education—the ones literate enough to make the best of the situation, but not so well educated as to view it as intolerable.

This was a brutal economic model. That sharecroppers were not far removed from slavery was also pointed out by H. L. Mitchell, one of the founders of the Southern Tenant Farmers Union, in his autobiography, *Mean Things Happening in This Land*. He describes what this life was like:

> For a sharecropper, the day started before dawn. The plantation bell was the first sound he heard upon awakening. His wife was soon getting a fire going in the cookstove. A cup of cheap coffee started the day off. She put biscuits in the oven to be eaten with molasses and fat back meat by the adults. There was cornmeal mush for the young ones. First the man would go to the plantation barn where the hostler assigned a mule to him. He harnessed it and was in the cotton field before sun was up. The day's work was well underway by sunrise, and it didn't end until after sundown. The plantation riding boss would be in the field supervising the croppers' work . . . In addition to seeing to it that each sharecropper was in the field and plowing his rows straight, the rider represented the law to both black and white sharecroppers alike. He replaced the slave driver of pre-Civil War days. The emancipation of the slaves put both black and white poor landless people to sharecropping—a new form of slavery.

Normally the work on the cotton plantations was well underway by March 1st. The land was first broken, then harrowed, and the rows were laid out for planting the cottonseed by the time the frost was out of the ground. March 1st was "Furnish Day," when the company store opened its doors to the sharecroppers to take on credit. Each family was entitled to draw its groceries and other supplies. There was a credit limit based on one dollar per month for each acre in cotton the cropper was to cultivate and harvest that year. The "furnish" was allowed only until the crops were laid by in July. Usually by about the 4th of July nearly all the work was done in the cotton fields, until picking time in the fall.

Cotton planting started in April. A single-row cottonseed planter was driven down each row in the field, dropping the seeds and lightly covering them. In a couple of weeks, depending on the weather, the cotton plants pushed through the soft crust of soil. When the plants were firmly set and up to the right height, the sharecropper took a special plow to scrape the weeds and dirt away from his cotton. Great skill was required to scrape the cotton on each side of the row, leaving the plants still with a firm foundation. Then the sharecropper's wife and all children old enough to chop came to the fields with long-handled hoes to thin the cotton to a stand. As it was chopped and thinned, the sharecropper used another plow to gently cover the row without destroying the plant.

The weeding of the cotton continued along with the plowing for at least six weeks. Everyone who was old enough to swing a hoe was needed to keep the field clean of weeds. The sharecropper kept his cultivator and his mule going from daybreak to dark. There would be a hurried meal in the middle of the day. Sometimes, if the work was going well, everyone had a short nap, resting on the shady side of the house . . . If a family was caught up with the work on its own piece of land, its members were often called upon to help other croppers who had fallen behind. Also, the owner might have a day-labor crop, where there was some extra work to be done. Usually there was a fixed wage for such work, 75 cents a day for grown folks, 40 cents for the young ones. I often worked chopping cotton back in Tennessee for 50 cents a day when I was growing up. By the time I was fifteen I was paid a man's wage . . . however, wages were seldom ever paid in cash. The family was just given credit for its account at the company store. Sometimes payment was made by printed pieces of paper to exchange for goods at the company store. These slips showed that the bearer was due the amount shown on the cover, and they came to be known as "doodlum books," or "due books." In some places they used pieces of brass: 1¢, 5¢, 10¢, 25¢, 50¢ and $1 pieces, good only at the company store. This money was known as "brozeene."

The prices at the company store were always much higher than those charged by the few small grocery store operators who managed to survive in town. In addition to the higher prices that the sharecroppers had to pay for basics such as flour, meal, and the fat back meat also called sowbelly, they were charged interest on the "furnish" they received. Usually this was 10 percent per month, on each dollar. An interest rate of 40 percent annually was considered normal . . .

After the crop was laid by in July, there was no more work for the sharecropper and his family until the last of September when the crop was ready to harvest. Naturally, credit was cut off at the commissary. It was a time for hunting, fishing, and going to "big meeting" where hellfire and damnation preachers held forth in the small churches of the black folks, and in hastily erected "brush arbors" for the white folks, which sheltered the sinners from the hot sun. All were there to repent their sins. Sometimes a white evangelist would come along who had his own tent. The plantation owners encouraged and often paid the preachers something extra to conduct the big meetings, so that field hands could hear their troubles blamed upon their sinful ways, rather than on the economic conditions under which they lived. . .

About the middle of September when the cotton started to open, the labor of every man, woman and child was needed in the harvest. Black and white, old and young were all in the fields. Schools, where they existed, always closed for "cotton picking time," . . . The same thing happened in the spring when schools were let out for "cotton chopping." . . . Children didn't get much learning anyway. As soon as a boy became strong enough, he became a plowhand and a valuable addition to the family economic unit. Since plowing was considered man's work, girls as a rule did not plow, so they got a little more schooling than the boys. Some girls even learned to read and write quite well.

The obstacles to education, especially for African Americans, are stated vividly by historian Robert J. Norrell: "In 1934 the expenditure for each white pupil in Macon County was $65.18 and for each black student $6.58. White teachers' salaries averaged $867 in 1934, as compared with $348 for blacks. White class enrollment averaged twenty-two students; black schools had almost sixty pupils in each class. County buses transported sixty percent of the white students to school, but no black children. Nearly seventy-five percent of black schools in the county in 1934 had only one teacher." And all this was, Norrell said, despite the participation in Macon County of the Rosenwald Fund. Julius Rosenwald was a white philanthropist from Chicago who became interested in education in the rural South after talking with Booker T. Washington. Rosenwald's money helped build a number of black schools in the rural South, and the very first was in Macon County. As we will see, Rosenwald's philanthropy played a role in the initiation of the Tuskegee Syphilis Study, too.

H. L. Mitchell's description of sharecropping continues:

> On some of the plantations, the sharecroppers were allowed to keep half of the money for which the seed was sold when their cotton was ginned. This was "cotton pickin' money." Sometimes black sharecroppers carrying their cotton to the gin to be baled were heard to say: "Git that white man's cotton off my seed."
>
> After the crop was all about picked out, usually just before Christmas, "settlement time" came. Sharecroppers would gather hopefully at the plantation commissary and the owner or his agent would call each man into the office in turn. The verdict would be handled down something like this: "Well, you had a good year. You raised twenty

bales of cotton. We sold it for seven cents a pound, that comes to $35 a bale, or a total of $700. Half of that is yours — $350. BUT you owe $200, plus interest of $80, on the furnish. You know we had to get the doctor when your wife was sick, and we deducted the doctor's calls and the medicines he gave, and then you bought some clothes for the children, too. The amount due you is $49.50. At least you got some Christmas money."

. . . Often the crop was not too good, or the sharecropper's account was over the amount the cotton brought when sold, and the man would then start the next year still in debt. He could not leave the plantation owing a debt. If he found a way to get his things moved at night, the law—usually the deputy sheriff—would be sent to hunt the man down and force him and his family to return. Sometimes a man's debt would be bought by another plantation owner, and the sharecropper would start off in debt to the new owner. Sometimes a planter to whom a sharecropper owed money would just pass out the word that the sharecropper was unreliable, and no one would let him have a place where he could make a crop. When that happened, his only hope was to find part-time work as a wage laborer, but that was a downward step to an agricultural worker.

H. L. Mitchell was a white man, and his personal experiences as a sharecropper were in Arkansas and Tennessee. But he organized for the Southern Tenant Farmer's Union in Alabama, too, and he gives a good account of what it was like across the South in this time period. Mitchell's union, though handicapped by charges that it was Communist-inspired, was a very interesting early example of organizing across racial lines, and some of its leaders later became active participants in the civil rights movement which developed in the forties and fifties. Ned Cobb was an African American farmer in the Notasulga area of Macon County whose involvement with Mitchell's union led to a violent 1932 confrontation with the law that was memorialized in the epic poem "In Egypt Land" by the Alabama poet John Beecher. From that poem, the author Ted Rosengarten later tracked Cobb down and further popularized his life, as "Nate Shaw," in the oral autobiography *All God's Dangers*. And Ralph Ellison describes life in Macon County during this era in his classic novel, *Invisible Man*.

For the purpose of examining the Tuskegee Syphilis Study, the point is that the men who were chosen as participants for this study came out of the cotton culture of the 1930s. They were for the most part very poor, not well educated, worked very hard in a cruel economic situation, and were by custom and social conditions accustomed to submitting to authority and uniforms, whether that uniform was that of the law or the white coats and dresses of doctors and nurses.

As for those doctors and nurses, health care in 1932 was largely inaccessible in Macon County. There were very few doctors in Macon County and only two hospitals. Macon County Hospital was exclusively used by whites, and John A. Andrew Memorial Hospital was located on the campus of Tuskegee Institute. Andrew Memorial Hospital's primary purpose was to provide health care for the students and officials of the College. It was also the center for providing health care for the local African American community, particularly for maternity patients, infant care, and treatment for tuberculosis. Dr. Eugene Dibble and Dr. Thomas Campbell were the only African American doctors in Macon County, and they were connected with John A. Andrew Memorial Hospital.

Historian Robert J. Norrell referred to sociologist Charles S. Johnson's research in Macon County. That research was part of a study financed by the Rosenwald Fund to study the extent of syphilis in the county. Norrell writes:

> Physicians working for the United States Public Health Service discovered in 1930 that thirty-six percent of fourteen hundred black men examined had the disease. They also found that health conditions for rural blacks in Macon County were miserable generally. Their diet consisted largely of salt pork, hominy grits, cornbread, and molasses; fresh meat, fresh vegetables, fruit, and milk were rarely included. Malnutrition was chronic, and they were afflicted by many diet-related illnesses. Most of the county's poor blacks could not afford medical care.

I have to point out that a similar survey would have found much the same thing if it had examined the poorest whites in the county, too, for their health conditions were not much better. However, a greater proportion of blacks were in these circumstances, and even the poorest whites did not carry the additional burden of legalized segregation. Nevertheless, in the thirties, most rural people simply did not have medical care. Children were born at home with their births assisted not by doctors but by midwives. Very few African Americans were treated by a doctor, and for African American males, the percentage was even lower. I am sure that only a handful of the 623 participants in the Tuskegee Syphilis Experiment, prior to being involved, had ever been treated by a physician. This was the state of health care in Macon County at the time the men were selected to enter the Experiment.

3

Origins of the Study

Syphilis was a terrible disease. It still is, of course, but it is easily treated today by a number of antibiotics. In 1932, that was not the case, and one can appreciate both the scientific zeal and the humanitarian instincts of those who originated the Tuskegee Syphilis Study at a time when there was no simple solution to what amounted to an epidemic among certain population groups.*

Before beginning work on this case, I, like most lay people, knew what syphilis was, but I knew little of the particulars of the disease. From the documents in this case and from talking with the medical professionals, I learned enough to explain that syphilis is caused by a bacterium, a spirochete, that lives only in humans and is almost always transmitted from one person to another by intimate sexual activity. However, congenital syphilis can also result when an infected pregnant women passes the disease to her developing baby, who can be born deaf, mentally retarded, blind, or with other disorders.

Once the syphilis bacterium is inside a person's body, the disease develops through three stages.

First, within ten to ninety days after infection, a small red pimple will

---

*The information in this chapter is drawn largely from documents and information discovered during the legal research for the court case filed in 1973.

appear at the site of infection, usually on the genitals. This pimple turns into a sore which is called a chancre. There is usually no pain or soreness and the victim may not even notice the chancre. In thirty to forty days, the chancre goes away.

The secondary stage begins about a week later and lasts for several weeks. The main visible sign is a rash that can appear, especially on the palms or the soles of the feet. Some people experience hair loss, fever, open ulcers, and headaches, while others have only very mild symptoms and may not even notice them. Any open ulcers during this phase are extremely infectious to others.

Between the second and third stages, there is a latent period which can last for years. During the latency, syphilis can only be detected by a blood test. Left untreated during this latent period, the third or late stage of the disease can occur at any time for the rest of the victim's life.

In the late stage, the syphilis bacterium attacks the neurological and cardiovascular systems of the body, damaging the heart, brain, and spinal cord, but also the skin, bones, and other organs. The victim's heart may fail, he or she may develop mental illness, may go blind and/or deaf, and may suffer paralysis, or other debilities. Although some people live to a ripe old age with syphilis and never have severe symptoms, others may be devastatingly ravaged by the disease. Persons with advanced syphilis may develop huge, encrusted ulcers on their skin, especially near their joints. Also, their brains may be affected to the point that they literally go stark raving mad. The bacterium also may attack the blood vessels or the heart, causing aneurysms that may burst, resulting in sudden death.

After Mr. Charlie Pollard came to see me in 1972 and I agreed to represent him in a lawsuit against those responsible for the Tuskegee Syphilis Study, my staff and I began to research the study's origins. As the case expanded, we included other researchers and the staffs of our associated counsels. Because the study had existed for so long, many of the original documents were filed away in long-forgotten archives. Gradually, the details emerged.

As mentioned in the previous chapter, the study began as a project of the Julius Rosenwald Fund, which took an active interest in both education and health care for African Americans in the rural South. Julius Rosenwald was a Jewish philanthropist who had helped build the Sears and Roebuck Company mail order business. He became a patron of Booker T. Washington and the Tuskegee Institute and also financed the construction of a large number of schools in parts of the South where state support for the education of African Americans was weak to non-existent; the very first of those schools was built in Macon County. Rosenwald's foundation sought to improve race relations in general as well as the specific health and social problems facing African Americans in the Southern states.

A large-scale public effort to combat venereal disease, including syphilis, had been underway in the U.S. since World War I, but in rural areas vast numbers of poor people were still unable to obtain any treatment. In Alabama, for example, some fourteen free clinics operated by the State Board of Health were treating ten thousand indigent patients by 1930. Yet most of these were in urban areas. In rural areas, the public health service gave private doctors free drugs for treatment of indigents, but the physicians were allowed to charge a two-dollar fee and many of the poorest patients could not afford that amount.

The Rosenwald Fund, meanwhile, sought an alliance with the U.S. Public Health Service (PHS) to expand medical services to the poorest African American areas of the South. In addition to its work in education and social services, the Fund was helping to build hospitals and clinics and was also promoting the hiring of African American nurses and doctors and the training and hiring of African American public health personnel. To oversee this work, Dr. Michael M. Davis was named medical director of the Rosenwald Fund. In 1929, Davis went to the surgeon general of the U.S. Public Health Service to ask for assignment of a PHS adviser to the Rosenwald medical efforts in the South. Dr. Taliaferro Clark, then head of the Public Health Service's Venereal Disease Division, a Virginian who had been with the Public Health Service since 1895, was given this assignment by then Surgeon General Dr. Hugh S. Cumming.

After appointing Clark as the Rosenwald adviser, Cumming then asked Davis for a Rosenwald grant to provide follow-up treatment for those found to be infected with syphilis in a testing program the PHS had just completed in Bolivar County, Mississippi. Approximately a fourth of the two thousand African Americans employed there by the Delta Pine and Land Company were infected.

Davis agreed to pay for a one-year program of treatments, provided that at least one African American nurse would be hired for the project. Thus the PHS was able to make a demonstration treatment program out of its survey project in Mississippi. The success of this effort led PHS officials to ask the Rosenwald Fund to help set up similar projects in other states. The Fund's directors subsequently appropriated fifty thousand dollars to be spent during 1930 for syphilis treatment demonstrations in six counties in Alabama, Virginia, Tennessee, Mississippi, North Carolina, and Georgia. The Alabama project was to be in Macon County.

Meanwhile, medical interest in syphilis in the early decades of the twentieth century was not limited to the South or even to the United States. Syphilis had been a serious health problem around the world for centuries. There was considerable research on syphilis throughout the world in the late nineteenth and early twentieth century as medical and scientific technology improved. The discovery of the causes and sometimes the cures of other diseases led medical professionals to hope a cure could be found for syphilis, too. The spirochete that actually causes the disease was isolated by two German scientists in 1905, and the Wasserman blood tests for detection of syphilis came along two years later. However, it would be another thirty-five years before the discovery of penicillin produced a reliable, effective cure.

During our legal investigation of the Tuskegee experiment, we found a document, "An Introduction to the Tuskegee Study," written in 1964 by R. A. Vonderlehr, M.D., for a venereal disease conference. This paper discusses some of the early research, beginning with a Norwegian study of 2,200 syphilis patients between 1891 and 1910. At the time, the only known treatment involved injections of arsenic-type drugs, which was not always effective and often caused serious side effects. The doctor doing the Norwegian study believed the patient's own immune system would be more effective. So he hospitalized these patients until their lesions healed but he did not treat them. Then, in 1928, the original doctor's assistant, Dr. E. Bruusgaard, reported on the fate of these patients during the fifteen to forty years since they had been infected. He found that of every "hundred patients with untreated syphilis, ten would develop neurosyphilis, thirteen cardiovascular syphilis, and twelve benign late syphilis, but that sixty-four would pass through life apparently unharmed. Furthermore, in twenty-eight of the sixty-four, 'spontaneous cure' would occur."

According to Vonderlehr, Bruusgaard's findings were considered suspect for various reasons of methodology, principally that he had obtained follow-up information on only 22 percent of the original 2,200 patients. Nevertheless, his report was received with great interest by syphilis specialists around the globe. During the years 1928-1930, the Health Section of the League of Nations—the forerunner of today's United Nations—conducted a survey, out of which a group of leading syphilologists of the day standardized a procedure for the treatment of early syphilis in the United States. Vonderlehr described both that treatment and the beginnings of the Tuskegee Syphilis Study:

> In general, this [standardized procedure] consisted of weekly injections of an arsenical and bismuth administered in alternating courses for a period of 70 weeks. For comparative purposes in evaluating the efficacy of this treatment, a group of untreated syphilitics was desirable. Although the Bruusgaard study had just been published, these data did not seem applicable to the situation in the United States. A large percentage of our infected population was Negro and with even our limited knowledge of that time we were aware that in this group syphilis more frequently attacks the cardiovascular than the central nervous system. We were also aware that although cardiovascular conditions could easily be detected their etiology could rarely be determined prior to autopsy.

Between 1929 and 1931 the Public Health Service in cooperation with local health departments and the Julius Rosenwald Fund had surveyed six rural areas in the South. The highest prevalence of syphilis (398 per 1,000) was found in Macon County, Alabama. Of the 1400 cases admitted to treatment during the survey, only 33 had ever had previous antisyphilitic therapy and the average for these 33 was less than 5 arsenical injections.

The large number of syphilis cases in Macon County, and the fact so few of the cases had received any treatment, was to play a crucial role in the creation of the Tuskegee Syphilis Study.

The Rosenwald/Public Health Service projects during 1930–31 were almost too successful. Approximately forty thousand persons were tested for syphilis in the six counties surveyed, and 25 percent were found to be infected. The infection rates ranged from a low of 7 percent in Albemarle County, Virginia, to a high of 36 percent in Macon County. Everyone involved realized they had documented a problem of enormous dimensions, and solving it would take both public money and public resolve. However, as the Great Depression deepened, there was less rather than more money available from both government and philanthropy to address the problem. The Rosenwald Fund directors, hamstrung by the declining value of the Fund's assets in the stock market, voted in the Spring of 1932 to end the syphilis treatment program.

However, as Dr. Vonderlehr indicates above, even if no funding was available for an ongoing treatment program, the very fact that there was so much *untreated* syphilis in Macon County offered the opportunity for a study of a different sort.

The idea for an observation study of the effects of untreated syphilis in Macon County may have originated with Dr. Taliaferro Clark, who was responsible for writing the report summarizing the Rosenwald surveys, or it may have come from some of the young white doctors who had worked on the project in Macon County. In any case, Dr. Clark became the high-level advocate necessary to create the Tuskegee Study of Untreated Syphilis in the Negro Male.

All the ingredients were there. The county had a high African American population (82 percent). The Rosenwald demonstration programs had shown the residents of Macon County to have the highest incidence of syphilis among the six counties surveyed in 1930–31. Virtually none of the cases of syphilis among the rural population had been treated. Thus, case acquisition, which required mass screening, could be done most cheaply here. In Tuskegee Institute's John A. Andrew Memorial Hospital, there was a facility where physical examinations, X-rays, and spinal taps could be made. PHS officials felt that the African American medical professionals associated with the Andrew Hospital were already known in the community and would help to reassure the African American subjects of the observation.

If there were no funds to treat the syphilis problem in Macon County, at least a scientific experiment might be a way to learn something from it, Dr. Clark reasoned. The study he proposed was not originally planned as a long-term observation of syphilitics. Clark's original design was for an observation project of only six to eight months. The goal was to assess the extent of medical deterioration, correlated against the duration of infection, among a group of untreated syphilitics. That group was to be located by mass screening a larger population using Wassermann tests. Like many public health surveys it was not single-purposed. Instead, the information gained would have helped answer a number of open questions of great interest. First, studies by American's leading syphilologist, Dr. J. E. Moore of Johns Hopkins, had shown that 80 percent of syphilitics would suffer active late lesions. However, the Bruusgaard study cited by Vonderlehr indicated that only 37 percent of those infected had developed active late lesions. Those patients had been left untreated by a doctor who doubted the efficacy of heavy metal treatments. If Bruusgaard was right, a 37 percent complication rate was interesting and might warrant questioning the benefit as opposed to the risk, of then current arsenical treatments.

Second, the venereal disease professionals of that era, like many medical researchers before and since, believed that government at all levels, and the public, misunderstood how important and deserving of support was their research. Reticence about discussing sexual matters, coupled with the high incidence of venereal disease among the poor, accounted for public indifference to what the doctors deemed, properly, one of the nation's major public health problems. If the true extent of the damage syphilis causes could be shown, the money for public health treatment efforts might materialize despite the Depression's onset. Third, poorly done studies of syphilis in African Americans showed the disease led to different complications than for Caucasians: African Americans endured much more heart disease, and considerably less paretic neurosyphilis. A properly conducted study could provide data on the incidence of the various types of late syphilitic complications among African Americans. The Bruusgaard study had involved only white Norwegians; the Rosenwald surveys promised a method of getting comparative data on black Americans.

Males were chosen for the survey because their sex organs are external. Males are much more likely than females to notice syphilitic chancres, and are therefore more likely to give an accurate medical history concerning the date of infection.

This was the Study plan. It was thought out from the scientific perspective, although its central premise, that reasonably accurate date-of-infection data could be obtained from the subjects, was known to be dubious at best. Otherwise, the Study was well designed to yield useful information. Its implementation was a disaster because almost no thought was given to the people who were to become its victims.

From the start the program was based upon making Macon County African Americans believe that this was another public health treatment program. The Rosenwald Foundation's earlier efforts had been enormously successful and had created a deep reservoir of good will among the local farmers and laborers. The Rosenwald files at Fisk University contain hundreds of appreciative letters and interview reports from Macon County residents.

This good will was systematically exploited in a manner perhaps never fully understood by the responsible government agencies. For example, Dr. Clark wrote that Macon County's high prevalence of untreated syphilis was a "ready-made situation, if I may be permitted to use this phrase," but "in order to secure the cooperation of planters in this section it was necessary to carry on this study under the guise of a demonstration and provide treatment for those cases uncovered found to be in need of treatment." That course, pretending that this was another Rosenwald-type demonstration and treatment program, was necessary not only to get the cooperation of the white planters, but also of the local African Americans.

From the beginning, the white doctors and public health officials involved knew that they were misleading the African American test subjects about the true purpose of their efforts in Macon County. Their correspondence and reports reveal that they knew they had to pretend to provide treatment in order to secure the participation of the African Americans to be tested, yet they had to *withhold* treatment in order to achieve their study results. As we shall see, they failed on both counts.

In the early fall of 1932, Dr. Clark traveled to Alabama to make preparations for the experiment. He met with several groups whose cooperation he felt was essential to the success of the program.

One group was the Alabama Board of Health and its director, state health officer Dr. J. N. Baker. Jim Jones, who assisted my legal team in researching the case, later wrote in his book *Bad Blood* that "Dr. Baker extracted an important concession from Dr. Clark in exchange for his approval and cooperation: Everyone examined and found to be syphilitic would have to be treated. How much treatment was the problem. Since Dr. Clark planned to finish the study within six to eight months, it would have been pointless for Dr. Baker to have insisted upon the full program of treatment necessary to cure syphilis. That required more than a year to complete." According to Jones, the understanding reached between Clark and Baker required "every patient who was examined and found to have syphilis, including those who were selected for the study, was supposed to receive eight doses of neoarsphenamine and some additional treatment with mercury pills, unless treatment with either drug was contraindicated on medical grounds."

Jones speculates that Dr. Baker had two primary motivations. First, giving at least minimal treatment for the Macon County syphilitics was the medically humane thing to do and, while it might not cure them, it would make them less contagious to others. Second, Dr. Baker knew that the "Rosenwald Fund's syphilis control demonstration had increased public awareness of what a menace the disease posed in the area. Dr. Baker may have reasoned that white employers would not cooperate unless the physicians offered some relief."

The support of white planters in Macon County was evidently considered important for getting out the word to the potential African American test subjects, but Clark did not meet with the planters on his September trip. That was left to the project staff once the work was actually underway.

Also key was to obtain the cooperation of Tuskegee Institute and the African American doctors at the Institute's Andrew Hospital. Both Dr. Eugene H. Dibble, the Medical Director of the hospital, and Dr. Robert R. Moton, the President of the Institute, permitted the government to use the facilities of the hospital for the Study. The PHS correspondence files indicate that surgeon general Hugh Cumming himself appealed for Dr. Moton's support, stressing the value to be gained from the research and the necessity of having the assistance of the doctors at Andrew Memorial Hospital.

A final group needing to be solicited for approval was the private physicians in the county. At that time, there were nine white and one African American physicians in private practice. According to PHS files, Dr. D. C. Gill, director of the state Bureau of Preventable Diseases, met on behalf of the PHS with the members of the Macon County Board of Health, the local medical association (in this period of segregation, the sole African American physician in the county was not allowed to be a member of the association). Gill explained the project to the association and the private doctors agreed to support it.

Meanwhile, Dr. Raymond Vonderlehr had been named by Clark as the Public Health Service officer who would actually be in charge of the Study. Like Clark, Vonderlehr was a Southerner (Virginia). He was in his mid-thirties at the time and had been with the PHS for a little less than a decade. He was well-respected by Clark and his other superiors and had an extensive background in syphilology, including cardiovascular syphilis.

Joining Vonderlehr to help launch the project was Dr. O. C. Wenger, the Director of the PHS Venereal Disease Clinic in Arkansas. Wenger had supervised the 1929 surveys in Mississippi that led to the Rosenwald surveys the next year, and he had accompanied Clark to Alabama in September 1932 to secure the cooperation of the Alabama Board of Health and Tuskegee Institute. He was certainly familiar with the goals of the project and well-qualified for the field work that was about to begin.

The PHS officials were interested in hiring an African American nurse for the project. Dr. Dibble recommended Eunice Rivers, who at that time was a supervisor of night nurses at Andrew Memorial Hospital. More than any other single person, Nurse Rivers was to personify the Tuskegee Syphilis Study to the six hundred men who became involved in it. For the purpose of the study, Nurse Rivers was assigned as a scientific assistant to Venereal Disease Program of the Macon County Health Department.

In any event, by October 1932, the U.S. Public Health Service, with the cooperation of public health agencies in Alabama, and the apparent approval of the local, state, and national medical establishments for treatment of venereal disease, was ready to embark upon a program which would *not* treat syphilis in African American males, in order to *observe* the effects of untreated syphilis. Thus the Tuskegee Syphilis Study was launched. It was to continue for forty years.

4

The Study, 1932–1972

The first phase of the Tuskegee Syphilis Study was the initial planned period of 1932–33, which was intended to collect a great deal of medical data about a group of men who had had syphilis for at least five years and had not been treated for it. Through blood work, spinal taps, physical examinations, and case histories of these infected men, Dr. Taliaferro Clark expected to gain valuable information for future syphilis treatment programs.

The second phase of the study began in 1933 when PHS officials most directly involved began to argue that the study should be extended indefinitely to see what else could be learned from its subjects. This argument required a rationalization that the minimal amount of treatment that had been necessary to win the cooperation of Alabama State Health Officer Dr. J. N. Baker in the first phase had not "contaminated" the study for the purpose of a longterm study of "untreated" syphilis. A control group of non-syphilitic men was also added during this period. Perhaps most significant, penicillin was discovered during this period but was withheld from the Study participants.

The third and final phase of the study began in the mid-1960s. The Study was by then three decades old, and it had evolved into virtually a tradition within the Public Health Service. However, a new generation of doctors was now involved, and it was a new era with a corresponding new awareness or even uneasiness of racial attitudes and civil rights activities.

While still not directly confronting the moral issues involved in the Tuskegee Syphilis Study, there was a growing sense that the original purpose of the experiment could no longer be defended as providing meaningful insights toward the future prevention and treatment of syphilis. The PHS officials in charge during the 1960s were having to evaluate ending the program or shifting its focus to a longterm study of aging. Neither solution addressed the problem of what to do with the men whose health had been compromised for all those years by denying them treatment.

Let us examine how the Study actually operated during these three phases.

Phase One: October 1932 to June 1933

In October 1932, word spread throughout Macon County that the "government doctors" who had provided free exams in 1930 were returning to start a new health program. Notices from Dr. Murray Smith and Nurse Eunice Rivers of the Macon County Health Department were circulated throughout the county by mail and at churches and schools. Dr. Smith was not yet working directly for the Study project, but it was conducted under the auspices of the county health department and Nurse Rivers was assigned to that department. These notices, incidentally, were the beginning of four decades of deception practiced on the six hundred African American males who were ultimately recruited for the Tuskegee Syphilis Study.

The first goal was to test enough patients to get a good study group. It had been determined that about four hundred infected males, twenty-five years or older, who had had syphilis for at least five years, would be needed for a scientifically valid study. The Rosenwald survey in 1930 had tested 3,684 African Americans of all ages and both sexes and had found 1,468 cases of syphilis. In 1932, a total of 4,400 men and women over eighteen years was tested, resulting in 990 positive cases. Of the overall test subjects, a total of 1,782 were males aged twenty-five and over, and of these 472 tested positive for syphilis. After further qualifying, 408 men with latent syphilis were selected for the Tuskegee Syphilis Study.

That was the goal and the methodology of the officials in charge of the program. From the point of view of the men involved, the goal was to obtain free health care, of which the first step was to take a blood test. Doctors and nurses administering the health program told the participants various things after blood tests were taken. Some of the participants were told they had "bad blood," however, they did not know what bad blood meant at that time. Others were told nothing. None was ever told he had syphilis. Most knew nothing about syphilis. They were not told they were involved in a study. They never gave or were even asked to give written consent.

Jim Jones notes in *Bad Blood* that to satisfy the condition of at least minimal treatment required by state health officer Dr. J. N. Baker, "syphilitics not included in the study had to be treated immediately after their diagnosis was confirmed, while syphilitics who were brought into the study could have their treatment deferred until after they were examined. Once the examinations were completed, however, they too had to be given treatment."

The actual field work in the fall of 1932 was conducted by Drs. Vonderlehr and Wenger with the assistance of Nurse Rivers and occasionally African American medical students or interns from Tuskegee Institute.

There was no problem obtaining blood tests. According to testimony given by Nurse Rivers in 1974, notice was given in churches, schools, through the county extension service, in stores, and generally spread by word of mouth. The notices listed the dates when the doctors would be at different locations, and a crowd would always be waiting. Some of the screening locations were in schools or churches; others were outdoors under shade trees. Nurse Rivers said she believed people showed up eagerly—even if, in some cases, they didn't know what a blood test was—because the screenings were something different in the routine of their daily lives, and out of the hope of receiving any kind of medical attention.

At the screening locations, Dr. Wenger, on loan to the project, took the blood samples, assisted by an intern from Andrew Hospital if one was available. Dr. Vonderlehr also took blood samples until enough positive results were obtained so that he could begin the physical examinations. This was the process: blood would be drawn and sent to the state health lab in Montgomery. If the test subject was male and twenty-five years old or older, a positive report for syphilis generated a notice for that person to come back for a second test. A second positive test generated a notice for the person to come in for a physical examination, which was conducted by Dr. Vonderlehr at the Andrew Memorial Hospital.

Nurse Rivers transported the men, two at a time, in her car to the hospital. Dr. Vonderlehr conducted two examinations in the morning, and two in the afternoon. The exams were thorough, including chest X-rays and electrocardiograms. He took detailed medical histories which further screened out those who had been previously treated for syphilis or whose infections were less than five years old.

Again, said Nurse Rivers, the prospect of *any* medical treatment combined with the novelty of the experience was enough inducement to get the men to come in for the physicals. She said, "In the early days, the people enjoyed the trip. It was a trip to town and a trip to Tuskegee Institute. They would come up and spend the day, two of them would get examined this morning and while those were getting examined, me any my buddy would go to town or go on the campus to see Tuskegee Institute because there were many that had not been to Tuskegee, even though they lived in Macon County. So they always looked forward to coming to Tuskegee and seeing us there."

Such comments indicate both the isolation of the rural participants in the Study and the physical obstacles which faced Nurse Rivers in her job of keeping in touch with the men and transporting them in the early years. In 1932, Macon County had only ninety-seven miles of paved roads, and the majority of those miles were on U.S. Highway 80 which ran through the county. During wet weather, the dirt roads turned into giant mudholes which made driving difficult if not impossible.

The screening and qualifying exams continued through the fall. By this time the agreement exacted by the state health officer for minimal treatment was placing an increasing demand on the project. A half-dozen clinics were opened in Macon County to treat syphilitic patients, and Dr. Murray Smith transferred from his job with the county health department to direct the clinics.

Although the treatment given in these clinics was indeed minimal, Dr. Vonderlehr felt the treatments had to be continued until the study was completed. In handwritten letters in January 1933, he wrote to Dr. Clark in Washington, "Our experiment cannot be carried out without treatments" and "It is my desire to keep the main purpose of the work from the Negroes in the county and continue their interest in treatment." That latter comment was another example of the deliberate intention to keep from the general public as well as the Study participants the fact that the purpose of the Study was to *observe* the effects of untreated syphilis.

However, the increasing cost of providing treatment and medical consultation to non-study participants led Vonderlehr to abandon churches and other community-based locations for screenings. This was due partly to the fact that women as well as men were showing up at the screening locations. Instead, the initial blood test screenings began to be taken from African American men who gathered at local Depression-era work projects and other such locations where few or no women would be present.

The screening, examining, and selecting of syphilitics continued into the Spring of 1933. In April and May, as the project neared the end of its work, it was time for the most difficult part of the medical process: the sampling of spinal cord fluid from "lumbar shots." This was a difficult and dangerous procedure, and Vonderlehr deliberately had postponed it to the end because he feared that once the spinal taps were carried out, many of the participants might quit the Study.

He was not wrong in his estimation of how the shots would be received by the men. According to Nurse Rivers, "The patient was placed on the table and bent over like this and the doctor inserted the needle in the spine and drew the fluid. It was a very, very cruel thing to do . . . very painful."

The purpose of the spinal taps was to allow the doctors to identify signs of neurosyphilis. Up to this point, the physical examinations had shown cardiovascular effects of syphilis, but virtually no effects on the central nervous system. If such symptoms were present, the spinal column fluid would show them.

The spinal taps were done with a three-inch needle inserted directly into the lumbar region of the spine. In the folklore of the Tuskegee Syphilis

Study that built up over the years within the Public Health Service, this process came to be known as "Vonderlehr's golden needle treatment." There can be little doubt that the spinal taps were extremely hard on the men. In later years Nurse Rivers spent a great deal of time reassuring the participants that no further spinal taps would be taken from them and that any present ailments they were having could not be blamed on the procedure.

According to Jim Jones in *Bad Blood*, Vonderlehr anticipated the effect on the project if word spread in the community about the spinal taps before they were completed on all the men. "Dr. Vonderlehr decided on a policy of bald deceit. He planned to assemble the men at the various field clinics and then transport them by automobile at the rate of twenty a day to Andrew Hospital, where the spinal taps would be performed and the men would be kept overnight for observation in case of adverse reactions."

That is how the taps were carried out during April and May 1933. Dr. Wenger was recalled from Washington to assist with the process, and the involvement of participants was encouraged further with a special letter giving the time and place each man was to meet Nurse Rivers for transportation to Tuskegee. "Remember, this is your last chance for special free treatment," Vonderlehr's letter proclaimed.

The fluid from the spinal taps was sent to government laboratories for analysis. That should have concluded the field research part of the Tuskegee Syphilis Study. However, Dr. Vonderlehr was not ready for the project to end. On April 8, 1933, he wrote to Dr. Clark:

> For some time I have been thinking of an aspect of the study of untreated syphilis being conducted here, which may not have occurred to you. I do not submit this idea with the desire that it even be considered a suggestion but rather that you keep it in mind until I return to my work in Washington.
>
> A the end of this project we shall have a considerable number of cases presenting various complications of syphilis, who have received only mercury and may still be considered untreated in the modern sense of therapy. Should these cases be followed over a period from five to ten years many interesting facts can be learned regarding the

course and complications of untreated syphilis. The longevity of these syphilitics could be ascertained, and if properly administered I believe that many micropsies could be arranged through the hospital at the Institute with the cooperation of the National Institute of Health. A part time social worker should be able to see the cases as often as necessary and the whole scheme could be supervised by one of our officers occasionally. Undoubtedly other interesting points for study could be worked out should this follow-up work be considered seriously. . . . It seems a pity to me to lose such an unusual opportunity.

Vonderlehr returned to Washington in June; Wenger returned to the PHS venereal disease section in Arkansas; Dr. Murray Smith went back to the county health department; and Nurse Rivers began cleaning up and closing the files. However, in June Dr. Taliaferro Clark retired, and Dr. Vonderlehr was named Acting Director of the PHS Division of Venereal Diseases. On July 18, Vonderlehr wrote to Wenger:

Dear Doc:

During the past 6 weeks I have been busily engaged in reviewing the literature in connection with our recent study of untreated syphilis in Alabama. I have also discussed the matter with a number of the officers here in Washington and everyone is agreed that the proper procedure is the continuance of the observation of the Negro men used in the study with the idea of eventually bringing them to autopsy. I realize that this may be impracticable in connection with some of the younger cases, but those more advanced in age with serious complications of the vital organs should have to be followed for only a period of a few years.

. . . I have reason to believe that this program will be approved by the Surgeon General. I am taking this matter up with you primarily to ascertain whether or not you have any member of your staff whose services could be dispensed without serious harm to the work at Hot Springs.

. . . Briefly my plan in Tuskegee is to obtain the cooperation of the State and local health departments and, most important of all, the Tuskegee Institute Hospital. Doctor Dibble would probably accept the appointment of Acting Assistant Surgeon at $1 per annum and act in an advisory capacity as far as the nurse was concerned. As you know, the nurse I plan to use is the previous one employed during the untreated syphilis project last winter, and I feel that we could employ her on a two-thirds basis, having her furnish transportation, for $1,000 a year. I believe that $200 per annum additional would furnish incidental needs, such as small amounts of medicines, et cetera.

The Study thus moved into a new phase, one that was to continue far beyond Vonderlehr's estimated "five to ten years" of additional observation and that, as we shall see, would bring into sharp focus in later years the issues of morality and medical ethics.

Phase Two: June 1933 to 1965

With the help of Surgeon General Cumming, Dr. Vonderlehr convinced Tuskegee Institute and its Andrew Memorial Hospital, the Tuskegee Veterans Administration Hospital, the Macon County Health Department, and the Alabama Board of Health to support the extended experiment. By October, Nurse Rivers was back on the Public Health Service payroll, still assigned to the Macon County Health Department, and working part-time on the Study. She also worked part-time in the Andrew Memorial Hospital in exchange for room and board at Tuskegee Institute.

The two most important immediate changes to the study were the addition of a control group of non-syphilitics and the plan to follow at least the older participants until they died, at which point autopsies would be performed so that direct clinical observation of the effects of the disease could be determined.

Dr. John Heller, who had joined the Public Health Service Division of Venereal Diseases about 1931, was appointed by Vonderlehr as the health officer to select and examine the control group. Dr. Heller had gone to medical school at Emory University, where he had been a classmate of Macon County health officer Dr. Murray Smith. Interestingly, Heller, originally from South Carolina, was, like Clark and Vonderlehr, another Southerner.

The control group of two hundred men similar in age and socioeconomic status to the four hundred syphilitics was selected from the men who had tested negative the previous fall. Again, these men were eager to receive "free" medical attention from "government doctors." During November and December 1933, and again in February and March, Dr. Heller performed blood tests and physical examinations until he had two hundred controls.

Arranging for the autopsies was more complicated and involved the elaborate social code of segregated Alabama. Vonderlehr and Heller sought the cooperation of all local and state officials who were involved in any way with issuing death certificates. They also wanted the cooperation of local physicians who might be called on to treat Study participants who were critically ill. To this end, Vonderlehr and Heller met with the medical societies of Macon and neighboring counties. The doctors in these societies were all white. In confidence, Vonderlehr told them the purpose of the Study and gave them lists of the participants.

Bringing the local white doctors into the project not only assured their cooperation with respect to reporting critical illnesses and deaths for the purposes of arranging autopsies, but it also put the Study participants on lists which kept them from inadvertently receiving treatment for syphilis.

The problem was to obtain autopsies on patients who commonly died without benefit of terminal medical care. The initial solution, having local doctors route hopelessly ill patients to Tuskegee for "free hospitalization," was a failure. Although both groups, syphilitics and controls, had received government letters telling them that free hospitalization would be provided in case of serious illness, most deaths occurred at home, and many subjects were buried without autopsies.

Then, in 1935, a burial insurance scheme was developed with the cooperation of the Milbank Memorial Fund, a New York foundation which supported medical research. Milbank provided a grant to allow payment of a fee (initially fifty dollars) for each autopsy. The fee was to be split between the doctor doing the autopsy and the family of the deceased. Nurse Rivers would offer burial insurance payment in exchange for the participants' families' cooperation with the autopsies. It was the only insurance most of them would ever have and provided a strong reason for the participant to stay in the program and for families to alert the project nurse when death occurred. The documentary evidence strongly suggests that African Americans were told of these new terms at the annual meetings held around the county in 1935. The doctors executed the scheme by informing the participants at the 1935 annual meetings that they wanted to evaluate and continue the bad blood treatment. Continued participation in the program would result in burial insurance. Also the government would treat other conditions disclosed by the physical exams. Dr. Vonderlehr wrote the Milbank Foundation on November 29, 1935:

> In addition to the measures aimed directly at autopsy study of these individuals, other work is carried on, the purpose of which is to retain interest in the project. The John A.. Andrew Memorial Hospital provides free hospitalization to all seriously ill patients included in this study. The Public Health Service employs a medical follow-up worker whose duty it is to visit each individual periodically. She also assists an officer of the Public Health Service who is detailed to Macon County at least once a year to examine and prescribe for those individuals who meet at a specified place.

The autopsies were conducted, and the samples of fluids and organs removed from the deceased participants were sent to the National Institute of Health. Nurse Rivers obtained the consent of family members for the autopsies. This was discussed in a 1953 medical journal article, "Twenty Years of Follow-up Experience in a Long-Range Medical Study," written by Nurse Rivers and several of the physicians of the U.S. Public Health Service: ". . . it was difficult for the nurse to approach the family, especially in the early years of the project, because she herself was uneasy about autopsies. She was pleasantly surprised to receive fine response from the families of the patients—only one refusal in 20 years and 145 autopsies obtained. Finally, the nurse realized that she and not the relatives had been hesitant and squeamish."

Thus the Study fell into a sort of routine. Nurse Rivers kept in regular contact with the participants, both syphilitics and controls, through visits and letters. Once a year, the men were given a blood test and "free medicine" was distributed. In 1932, 1938, 1948, and 1952, young Public Health Service doctors came from Washington for re-surveys. The men were brought to Andrew Memorial Hospital for complete physical examinations, though the dreaded "golden needle" spinal taps were never again administered. When a participant died, Nurse Rivers would secure permission for the autopsy, the procedure would be carried out, and the samples sent to Washington.

Maintaining the long-term cooperation of the participants was important, and over the years various inducements were used.

Some participants were promised free hot lunches and free transportation to be examined. The methods used to induce participation in the study are best described in Nurse Rivers's 1953 article, mentioned above:

> Because of the lower educational status of a majority of the patients, such as farmers and day laborers, it was impossible to appeal to them from a purely scientific approach. Therefore, various methods were used to maintain and stimulate their interest: free medicine, except penicillin; burial assistance or insurance (the project was referred to as "Miss Rivers' Lodge"); free hot meals on the day of the examination by public health service physicians periodically, transportation to and from the hospital, and an opportunity to stop in town on the return trip to shop or visit with friends.

In 1958, the participants were given another incentive in the form of an elaborately printed twenty-five year certificate of participation signed by the Surgeon General and accompanied by twenty-five dollars, one dollar for each year of the Study.

To most of the participants, the novelty of the medical attention was itself an incentive. Nurse Rivers testified in a deposition in 1974 that "when these men were brought in, it was just like you would be thinking about going to New York with them, to get a chance to come to Tuskegee and spend the day . . . It meant everything in the world to have the patient get a physical examination. Because, a lot of times they would tell me, Mrs. Rivers, what do he put that thing on your chest for. And I said that is to tell your heart. And they would say, you can tell your heart like that. And they were somebody. Here was a group of men out of a community where folks had never seen any doctor and this was—they were really somebody to have somebody give that kind of attention to them."

At the annual blood tests, syphilitics and controls alike were given various shots, a green-colored iron tonic, and pink pain pills that were actually aspirin. Virtually none of those interviewed in later years knew the purpose of the shots, but assumed they were for "bad blood."

"Well, they were very happy with whatever they were getting," Nurse Rivers testified in 1974 about the medical attention that had been offered to the participants over the years.

That medical attention compromised the participants' health, however, in the critical area of treatment for the very disease—syphilis—that had brought them to the attention of the U.S. Public Health Service in the beginning.

Jim Jones writes in *Bad Blood:*

> Under the dynamic leadership of Dr. Thomas Parran, who succeeded Dr. Cumming as surgeon general in 1934, the United States launched a vigorous nationwide syphilis campaign in the late 1930s. Building upon what had been learned during the Rosenwald Fund demonstrations, the PHS covered the nation with a Wassermann dragnet. The campaign reached whites and blacks alike, as mass testing and mobile treatment clinics introduced a bold new program of public health work in the United States.
>
> . . . Yet Dr. Parran's national campaign never reached a select group of African American men in Macon County, Alabama. Years before the program began, the PHS had sealed them within a scientific experiment that systematically cut them off from all treatment programs for syphilis—whether conducted by local, state, or federal health officials.

It is unclear from the record whether it was during this anti-syphilis campaign in the late 1930s or a later similar campaign sometime in the late forties or early fifties, after the development of penicillin, that there was a major effort to get all persons in Macon County with syphilis treated. Most of the whites and many blacks were sent to Birmingham to receive such treatment. However, those who participated in the Tuskegee Study were not permitted to receive such treatment. Herman Shaw, one of the participants, recalls that he was included in a group of men who were taken to Birmingham for treatment.

During the night before they were to be treated, a lady who was in charge of the facility where they were staying was pacing the floor. He asked her, "Ma'am, what's the matter?" She said, "There is somebody who is here that's not supposed to be here." He said, "Who is it and what's his name?" She said, "Herman Shaw." He said, "I'm Herman Shaw." She said, "You're not supposed to be here. Get up and put on your clothes."

He followed her instructions, they put him on a bus, sent him home and never treated him.

Similarly, a mobile treatment program began operating within Macon County. Locally, this was referred to as the bad blood wagon. Nurse Rivers, as part of her duties as a county health nurse, participated in this program. By this time, lists of all Study participants were well-circulated to area physicians, funeral homes, and probably to local white employers. Nurse Rivers was reluctant to testify about this in her 1974 deposition, perhaps out of concern that she might be herself liable or perhaps not wanting to reflect badly on the PHS, her employer of three decades. However, she did admit that when Macon County residents lined up for treatment by the "bad blood wagon," participants in the Study would be identified from lists or by her and those men would not be treated.

Similarly, the white doctors, whom Vonderlehr and Heller painstakingly tried in 1933 to make feel that they were a part of a scientific study, excluded Study participants from direct treatment for syphilis and perhaps even from indirect treatment by penicillin for other illnesses. And during World War II large numbers of rural Alabamians of both races were pulled from their isolation by the military draft. Physical examinations and medical treatment were routine features of the induction process and any Study participants who were drafted were likely to receive penicillin treatments. On August 6, 1942, Dr. Murray Smith wrote to Dr. Vonderlehr about the problem:

> A new situation has arisen with reference to the untreated syphilis study patients. Some of the Control cases who have developed syphilis, are getting notices from the draft boards to take treatment. So far, we are keeping the known positive patients from getting treatment. Is a control case of any value to the study, if he has contracted syphilis? Shall we withhold treatment from a control case who has developed syphilis? Please let me have your wishes with reference to handling this type patient and I will carry them out as best as I can.

The issue of withholding treatment, especially after the development of penicillin, was a major factor in the ethical questions that began to be raised over the Study in the mid sixties. Astonishingly, up to that point, there is little in the public record to indicate that anyone, from the PHS, the Milbank Memorial Fund, or Tuskegee Institute raised significant moral or ethical concerns about the Tuskegee Syphilis Study. The closest to an expression of concern over the welfare of the men in the PHS files is in remarks prepared by Dr. Oliver Wenger for presentation at a venereal disease seminar in September 1950.

This is a very interesting document, which I quote in its entirety:

> Untreated Syphilis in Negro Male
>
> Dr. Wenger
>
> Hot Springs Seminar
>
> In this series of meetings there has been much discussion about finding people with syphilis, how to treat them and how to evaluate the results of that treatment. This is good and it is proper. But in the few minutes I have, I wish to focus your attention on another aspect of the broad study of syphilis,—that of its affect on those you don't find, don't treat and don't follow.

This subject of untreated syphilis is not something new. The study of it was started some twenty years ago and has been plodding quietly along ever since, with parts of the findings coming to print sporadically. I would like briefly to review the matter.

Among the many interests of the late Julius Rosenwald was the health and welfare of the American Negro. From the Fund that now carries his name came money which was used in cooperation with Federal, State and local health departments for a survey of the prevalence of syphilis among negroes. One county in each of six southern states was chosen for study. The highest rate was found in Macon County, Alabama. Not only was the prevalence higher, but it was found that only one out of 25 had received treatment. With this as a start, Drs. Vonderlehr, Heller, Taliaferro Clark, Austen Diebert and myself, along with others, got together to organize a study of the syphilitic process when uninfluenced by treatment and to compare those findings with results after treatment had been given.

We decided to limit the study to negro males 25 years old or more. In the winter months of 1931–32 and 32–33 a group of 399 negro males with untreated syphilis was selected together with a group of 201 negro males who were presumably non-syphilitic to be used as a control. The age distributions in the two groups were comparable.

I won't bother you with minor details of how the study was to operate except to say that all were to have regular blood tests, and physical examinations. In addition it was planned to secure autopsies at death whenever possible. The Milbank Memorial Fund agreed to contribute money for necropsy. Part of the money goes to the physician doing the work and part of it goes to the family to aid in burial expenses.

The first physical examinations were made in 1932–33 with the findings published in September 1936. In 1938–39, a second physical examination was made at which time it was found that a considerable proportion of the younger men had received some but inadequate treatment.

From the second examination came two papers in 1946—one

covering mortality, in February, and one on cardiovascular abnormalities and other forms of morbidity, in December.

A third physical examination was made in the fall of 1948. In May of this year, 1950, the findings were published, covering abnormalities observed over 16 years.

Now, what have these findings been, in terms of generalities? First, that untreated syphilis apparently shortens the life expectancy by 20 percent. Second, that there is a greater involvement of the cardiovascular system and third, that syphilitics without treatment appear to be subject to a higher rate of other types of morbidity. Thus there are more potentially disabling defects among them and they die earlier. This is probably what most people might expect from general knowledge or assumption, but it is important to have the facts documented.

I heartily support the work that has been done, but it does not go far enough. When the third examinations were done in 1948–49, 26 percent of the syphilitics had been lost from observation and 35 percent of the controls. This is not counting known deaths. One of the reasons for selecting Macon county as a study area, aside from its high prevalence rate, was that it seemed remarkably suitable for the study purposes. It had the broad extremes of development of the Negro race, from those connected with Tuskegee Institute to those with the lowest of living standards. Health facilities ranged from a Veterans hospital to nothing, transportation from 3 railway centers and a main highway to inaccessible winter roads. But most of all, the county's principal industry is agriculture of a type which tends to provide a stable population for a long term study such as this. What became of this third or so that dropped from observation? Were they in the county but just didn't respond to a written notice? Would they have responded if they could read? Did they stay away because they were no longer interested or were they too ill to come in? Perhaps they had moved out of the county. Some have, I am sure. But if they've moved—are they living and well? If they are dead, what was the cause?

These questions are important to the value of the study. There is a nurse in the county whose salary is paid to keep track of these patients but I think more is necessary. Remember, these patients wherever they are, received no treatment on our recommendation. We know now, where we could only surmise before, that we have contributed to their ailments and shortened their lives. I think the least we can say is that we have a high moral obligation to those that have died to make this the best study possible.

This is the last chance in our country to make an investigation of this sort. You may say, if that's so isn't the point rather academic. I don't think so. It may be academic so far as the patient who is treated, but you know even better than I, that you are not yet finding and treating all of the cases. Your case finding publicity makes a point for the public to "Know for Sure" whether the disease has been contracted. I say it behooves the medical profession to "Know for Sure" what happens if the disease is not treated.

I urge in the strongest possible way that the Public Health Service place a full time male investigator in Macon county whose sole job is to locate those persons who were first selected and examined. Sure, they may have moved, perhaps moved and died, but arrangements can be made for them to be examined wherever they may be, if living. If they've died, let's trace them through vital statistics to see when, where, and why. And if humanly possible, arrange for autopsy of those who die in the future.

This matter of autopsies is of tremendous importance. There are, as you know, only two other studies that even remotely resemble this—the one started by Bruusgaard in Norway and the study of Rosakn at Yale. So far, of the 173 deaths recorded for the Alabama group, 67 percent have come to autopsy. The correlation of postmortem findings with periodical clinical findings can be done only in the Alabama group. What other way will we ever be able to learn the meaning of our clinical findings?

Once again let me emphasize the importance of this quiet undertaking and urge that steps be taken so that it doesn't slip through our fingers.

I noted earlier that Dr. Wenger's impassioned seminar speech in 1950 was the closest in the PHS record to an expression of moral concern about the Study. However, his concern is really aimed, not at the welfare of the participants, whose lives he admits have been shortened by lack of treatment, but the emphasis is on getting the maximum amount of data from the study.

Can there be any wonder that the men involved in this Study, when they learned what had been done to them, felt like "human guinea pigs?"

The Final Phase: 1965 to 1972

I have used 1965 somewhat arbitrarily as the beginning of the end of the Tuskegee Syphilis Study. By this time a new generation of doctors was involved. Nurse Rivers had gone into semi-retirement. Four to five hundred of the original six hundred participants had died. More significantly, the climate of race relations had changed dramatically over the three decades since the beginning of the Study.

As described in Chapter 2, in 1932 segregation was rigidly enforced and Jim Crow was the law of the land. By the end of 1965, Alabama had experienced a substantial change in race relations. On May 17, 1955, the United States Supreme Court's *Brown* decision destroyed the doctrine of "separate but equal," and held that separate elementary and secondary schools for black and white children in America were unconstitutional. This was the first major blow against legalized segregation based on race. Seventeen months later, on December 1, 1955, Mrs. Rosa Parks was arrested for refusing to give up her seat to a white man on a city bus in Montgomery, Alabama. On December 5, 1955, she was convicted and fined ten dollars in municipal court and that was the beginning of the Montgomery Bus Boycott. Most historians agree that her arrest and the subsequent rise of leadership of Dr. Martin Luther King, Jr., through the Montgomery Bus Boycott marked the beginning of the modern Civil Rights Movement.

In Tuskegee, from the early 1940s, African American leaders in Macon County, like Dr. C. G. Gomillion and William P. Mitchell had waged a massive effort to obtain the right to vote. On August 25, 1945, they had filed the early voting rights case *Mitchell v. Wright*. Their ongoing fight for the right to vote in Macon County spans from 1942 to the passage of the Voting Rights Act in 1965. Study participant Charlie Pollard was a community leader from the Notasulga area who worked with Dr. Gomillion and Mr. Mitchell to obtain the right to vote.

In 1958, there was an upcoming municipal election in Tuskegee. To prevent African Americans from voting, a bill was passed in the Alabama Legislature which changed the city limits of Tuskegee, thus excluding substantially all of the registered African American voters in the City of Tuskegee but leaving on the rolls all of the white voters. This gerrymandering of the city boundaries had two results: (1) African Americans decided to stop trading with the white merchants in downtown Tuskegee. As a part of a selective buying program, they had mass meetings once a week similar to what happened in Montgomery during the Montgomery Bus Boycott. (2) I was retained by the Tuskegee Civic Association to bring legal action against that legislative gerrymandering. I filed the lawsuit *Gomillion v. Lightfoot*. This case ultimately reached the United States Supreme Court, the act was declared unconstitutional, African Americans were able to vote in city elections, and the entire political power structure in Macon County during this time was changing from all white to substantially all black.

During this same era, I filed *Lee v. Macon County Board of Education*. This precedent-setting case began as a lawsuit to desegregate the public schools in Macon County and later was expanded to include desegregation of all the elementary and secondary school systems — a total of ninety-nine systems—in the State of Alabama not already under court order in other cases. About the same time that the gerrymandering bill passed the Alabama Legislature, Attorney General John Patterson filed a lawsuit which enjoined the NAACP from doing business in the State of Alabama. Patterson's purpose was to prevent and delay integration in Alabama. Ultimately, it took eight years of litigation before the NAACP was able to return to the State of Alabama. Patterson's racial views and racially motivated actions, of course, made him so popular with white voters that he was elected governor in 1958, defeating a *more moderate* George C. Wallace.

During this period of time, many other cases and civil rights efforts were destroying segregation in and outside of Alabama. The point is that there were substantial differences in how people felt about race in Macon County in 1965 and what they believed in 1932. Notwithstanding these changes in attitude and the change of the political structure from white to black, the infamous Tuskegee Syphilis Study continued and was still generally unknown to the public. However, the persons who were administrating the program in the mid-sixties began to be very concerned about what would happen if and when the Study was revealed. On the other hand, even during the final phase between 1965 and 1972, they would not face up to the racial issues involved. In an April 1965 meeting, several Public Health doctors and the Center for Disease Control discussed the Study. The only reference in the minutes with respect to race is, "Racial issue was mentioned briefly." The minutes further stated that "it would not affect the Study. Any questions raised could be handled by stating that the people were at the point that the therapy would no longer help them."

The conductors of the Study ignored the racial implications of the Study. As will be observed later, one of the key issues when the story became known was that the Study was racist. President Clinton in his apology stated that "the Study was clearly racist."

Although the Study seemed to be completely unaffected by the guidelines that arose from the post-World War II Nuremberg trials, there was continuing discussion on human experimentation within the overall scientific and medical communities. In 1964, the World Health Organization published the Declaration of Helsinki which introduced guidelines on the ethics of human experimentation. That same year a report of the National Institute of Health focused attention on the lack of controls on clinical research involving humans within the U.S. And in 1966, Policy and Procedure Order 129 was issued by the Surgeon General to define the PHS procedures on clinical research.

According to Jim Jones, who located the PHS records that I used in the lawsuit on behalf of the Study participants and for his book, *Bad Blood*, "none of the guidelines contained provisions that applied to the PHS's own research programs. . . . Thus none of the health officers connected with the Tuskegee Study expressed any ethical concern until critics started asking questions." Jones identifies the first of these critics as Dr. Irwin J. Schatz of Detroit, who wrote to the PHS in 1965 after reading a 1964 report on the study coauthored by Dr. Anne Yobs. Schatz was "utterly astounded by the fact that physicians allow patients with a potentially fatal disease to remain untreated when effective therapy is available."

Yobs did not reply to Schatz's letter, but she had been a part of a "Meeting Re: Tuskegee Study" in April 1965 in which several doctors from PHS and the Centers for Disease Control discussed what to do with the data from the Study. According to notes summarizing the meeting, Dr. Yobs observed, "If you can't evaluate it somehow, you better call it quits right now because it is not getting any clearer as time goes on."

The minutes of the meeting state, in part:

> In evaluating this study, it is no longer untreated late latent syphilis. . . . Further evaluation of the remaining patients was discussed. Dr. Olansky said he would hate to see us lose them now. Thinks we should follow them till death do us part. . . . The need for a second nurse to be assigned there to take over when Nurse Rivers is gone was discussed. If we don't have another nurse there to take over, the study will come to an end. . . Racial issue was mentioned briefly. Will not affect the study. Any questions can be handled by saying these people were at the point that therapy would no longer help them. They are getting better medical care than they would under any other circumstances. The consensus was the study should definitely be continued.

Again, no one within PHS was raising specific moral questions about the Study, but there was what seemed to be a new awareness of its sensitivity and its vulnerability to criticism. By 1969, internal PHS sensitivity about the Study had increased, in part due to a new critique which was being raised by former PHS venereal disease investigator Peter Buxtun. In the next chapter, we will examine Buxtun's key role in bringing the study to a close, but his critical questions beginning in 1966 certainly were a factor in prompting the establishment of an ad hoc committee to review the Tuskegee Syphilis Study.

The committee met in Atlanta on February 5, 1969, for a discussion convened by Dr. David Sencer of the National Communicable Disease Center. (The NCDC was the new name of the Venereal Disease Division of the Public Health Service.) The committee was composed of Dr. Gene Stollerman of the Department of Medicine, University of Tennessee, Memphis; Dr. Johannes Ipsen Jr. of the Department of Community Medicine, University of Pennsylvania, Philadelphia; Dr. Ira Myers, Alabama Health Officer, Montgomery; Dr. J. Lawton Smith, Ophthalmology Department, University of Miami; and Dr. Clyde Kiser, Milbank Memorial Fund, New York. Non-committee members present included Dr. Sidney Olansky of Emory University, formerly with PHS; and Dr. William J. Brown, then head of the PHS Venereal Disease Division.

According to the official minutes of the meeting, after giving a brief historical summary of the Study, Dr. Sencer got right to the point:

> Dr. Sencer then said the question has come up: Should we terminate the Study or should we continue it? It becomes a political problem. At the time the Study was begun there was no concern about racial problems, discrimination, etc. At that time there was no problem about not treating the disease. "We want your advice in making a decision. We are here to discuss this problem."

There followed lengthy discussion of diagnoses, pathology reports, survival rates, ages of the living participants, autopsy findings, and the methodology of the Study itself.

> Dr. [J. Lawton] Smith said serological and epidemiological workups were good. The weak link in the chain is pathology. He suggested tremendous emphasis be put on this study, in the next few years the patients are going to be gone. . . . "First, stress pathology; get away from serology. You will never have another study like this; take advantage of it." . . . "This is a golden moment. Turn this study into pathology studies."
>
> Dr. Stollerman thought there was a moral obligation here to treat

patients for neurosyphilis. The participants then discussed the dangers of treatment—Herxheimer reactions, fibrillations, etc. Dr. Stollerman thought we were obliged to set criteria for treatment. Dr. Olansky said if we insisted on spinal taps we would not have any patients.

Dr. Sencer asked the Alabama Health Officer about the Macon County medical society, to which Dr. Myers responded that it had completely changed. At the beginning of the study in 1932 the local doctors had all been whites, now there was only one white doctor in the county and five to seven African American doctors. The minutes note, "He said they had been very reasonable to work with; some of the fears of real troublemaking have not come to pass."

Dr. Dull then asked how you could answer criticisms for not treating these patients. Dr. Sencer said if we established good liaison with the local medical society, there would be no need to answer criticisms.

Dr. Myers said at this stage he thought we should only take better care of the patients. Dr. Smith recalled when he was there in 1967 he found two cases of glaucoma and brought them to treatment. If he had not, they would have gone blind. "I think the patients appreciate this."

Dr. Olansky reiterated that the original policy of the Study was that when medical treatment was indicated, they were pulled out of the Study and given treatment.

Dr. Myers stated that Macon County is now being promoted as a Negro center of culture. "I don't know where you will be able to study this kind of group. No populations are that stable these days. These patients are over 70; they do not move anymore."

The discussion continued at some length, covering a need to find someone to replace the aging Nurse Rivers, to increase financial support to the project both to improve the autopsy process and to care for the various health needs of the participants, and to open up new relationships with the doctors now practicing in the area. Dr. Stollerman continued to press for treatment of the individuals involved, noting "I think you should treat each individual case as such, not treat as a group."

Dr. Kiser of the Milbank Fund spoke up: "This is not a Study that would be repeated now. The public conscience would not accept it. . . . I am impressed with the plan, but I don't know if the Fund would up the ante."

> Dr. Sencer then said he thought everyone understood the sense
> of what we wanted to accomplish, "and we are going to do it. We will
> lean heavily on [Dr.] Ira [Myers]."

Thus ended the most intense self-examination of the Study of which records were found in the PHS files up to that point. Following the meeting, attendee Dr. Clyde Kiser of the Milbank Memorial Fund wrote colleague Alexander Robertson a summary report:

> . . . Doctor Sencer explained that the purpose of the Ad Hoc
> Committee was to discuss whether the Study should be terminated or
> continued. If it is to continued what changes if any should be made?
> He stated that the political as well as the moral aspects of the Study
> should be considered. For instance, under State Law the "informed
> consent" of people is required if they are subject to investigation, medi-
> cal tests, etc. The educational level of the Negroes in the Study is so
> low that it would not be possible to explain "informed consent" to
> them.

Kiser noted that Sencer made a point of telling committee members the NCDC did not have preconceived opinions as to the future course of the Tuskegee Study, welcomed all opinions, and would be guided by the recommendations of the group. Kiser's report went on to review briefly the history of the Study and the Milbank financial support—"$16,500 for the years 1935–1965"—over the years. He continued:

It should be emphasized, however, that the syphilitic-control dichotomy is not water tight. During the course of the years some controls contracted syphilis and almost all the syphilitic subjects had at least some type of treatment on their own. It was also emphasized that the Wassermann & Kahn tests have been superseded by more adequate tests, such as the Treponema Pallidum Immobilization (TPI).

In general, the last round-up results of both the recent decedents and the survivors have emphasized similarities of the syphilitic and control groups. This was in sharp contrast to the results of the 12 reprints of studies that we have on the Tuskegee Study. Even [the most recent article in the Milbank files, from 1964] contained the statement: "By 1952, after twenty years of follow-up, 40 per cent of the syphilitics and 20 per cent of the controls had died; at this time the life expectancy of individuals from ages 25 to 50 with syphilis was determined to be reduced by 17 per cent."

. . . As for the future of the Study, there was acknowledgment first of all that a Study of this type would never be repeated. Public conscience would not condone carrying a group of people through lifetime with untreated syphilis. It was stated, however, that at the time the Study was instituted the facilities for getting treatment were remote. Penicillin had not yet been discovered. Furthermore, there probably would have been resistance to treatment on the part of the poorly educated rural Negro males in Alabama.

. . . Doctor Sencer's synthesis of the meeting was approximately as follows: There is merit in continuing the Study. He has not been impressed that treatment of the Study group is indicated as a routine procedure for the future. However, individual cases where treatment is needed should be treated or offered treatment. It is essential to establish liaison with the local Health Department in Macon County, Alabama and to enlist their cooperation in furthering the Study. It may be necessary and desirable to subsidize a full-time person to work with the local Health Department and with the local Medical Group of Negro doctors.

In the aftermath of the Atlanta ad hoc committee meeting, the PHS with the help of Dr. Myers and his staff in Alabama developed a new working relationship with the Macon County Medical Society and with the staff of Andrew Memorial Hospital at Tuskegee Institute. In April 1970, Nurse Elizabeth M. Kennebrew was hired to replace Nurse Rivers. She and the others involved in the Study at that point tried hard to locate participants who had been missing from the Study in recent years.

The next round of inquiry about the Tuskegee Syphilis Study would be external rather than internal, and the end of the project was in sight.

5

The Study Revealed

It was not until the summer of 1972 that the surviving participants learned through the news media that they were part of the Tuskegee Study. From the time the Study started in 1932 until this disclosure, the public in Macon County generally had absolutely no knowledge about the Tuskegee syphilis experiment. True enough, there were a few doctors connected with John A. Andrew Memorial Hospital and the Veterans Administration Medical Center in Tuskegee who had some knowledge of the program. Some doctors were familiar with the periodic examinations of the participants in the experiment. Some performed autopsies. It was later revealed that local doctors in Macon County and the surrounding counties had been given lists of men who were not to be provided penicillin treatments for syphilis.

However, the individuals who had specific knowledge about the Study were very few, and the public generally had no such knowledge. I had practiced law in the State of Alabama, Montgomery, and Macon County since 1955. I considered myself to be knowledgeable about most matters affecting those counties, including health care. I was very active in Macon County and had been involved in civil rights litigation there since 1956 beginning with the selective buying campaign by the Tuskegee Civic Association, the gerrymandering case *(Gomillion v. Lightfoot)* that I argued and won before the U.S. Supreme Court, a lawsuit to end discrimination in jury selection, substantial work in the area of voter registration, another lawsuit to end racial discrimination in federally supported agriculture programs, and a lawsuit to integrate the public schools in the county. However, despite my civic, church, legal, and political involvement in Macon County, I was like other citizens in that I had no knowledge at all about the Tuskegee Syphilis Experiment.

Although data from the Study were sporadically reported in medical periodical literature, the general public knew nothing about it until the Associated Press ran a widely distributed news report in July 1972.

How this wire service report came about is an interesting story in itself.

Public Health Service employee Peter Buxtun was working in San Francisco in the mid-1960s as a venereal disease interviewer and investigator. Through his work, he rather incidentally heard about the Study. What he heard surprised and shocked him. Buxtun became very, very concerned and had some questions in his mind about these men not being treated and the whole manner in which the Study was being conducted. By this time, scores of PHS doctors and other staff members had been involved in the Tuskegee Study for more than three decades. Medical journals had been publishing periodic reports, presumably read by thousands of doctors and medical researchers, for these three decades. However, Buxtun and Dr. Irwin J. Schatz of Detroit, mentioned in the previous chapter, were evidently the first whose ethical sensitivity compelled them to realize that the Study was simply wrong and to speak out.

Schatz wrote a single letter to Public Health Service officials; he received no response. I don't know whether Schatz took any other action. Buxtun, however, though the Tuskegee Study was taking place three thousand miles away and really did not concern his particular duties with the PHS, decided to get involved. He obtained copies of the previously published reports on the Study, and, evidently the more he learned of it the more concerned he became.

Buxtun later wrote in a prepared statement about his role:

> I was shocked by statements such as: "An important phase of the study has been the performance of autopsies" . . . ". . . mortality and morbidity are consistently higher among the untreated syphilitics,"

and other passages which indicated the participants did not realize what was happening to them. . . .

Upon reflection, I excerpted sections from these reports and from other sources (including the Proceedings of the International Military Tribunal, Nuremberg) into an attack upon the moral justification for the study. I pointed out that the Tuskegee study could be compared to the German medical "experiments" at Dachau and that public disclosure of such a scandal could jeopardize Congressional funding for other, beneficial PHS projects.

My superiors were shocked at what I had done, but after warning me that I would probably be fired, they agreed to forward my report to CDC. . . . The initial reaction seemed to be shocked silence.

Fearing that his report would not attract attention within PHS, on November 9, 1966, Buxtun wrote to Dr. William J. Brown, then chief of the Venereal Disease Division of the PHS:

It is my understanding that the study of untreated syphilis in the negro male has been supervised by your department. I am also given to understand that over thirty years ago a group of negro syphilitics was programmed for a special study, and that these men were given either insufficient or placebo treatment. Furthermore, I am told that these men are not volunteers, but were (and are) told that they were receiving proper treatment.

I am impelled to ask: 1) was this study initiated to obtain physical examinations and autopsy reports on the syphilitic damage which these men were being allowed to endure? 2) Have any of these men been fully treated? 3) Have any of these men been told the nature of this study? 4) Is the study still underway? In other words are untreated syphilitics still being followed for autopsy?

Your attention in the above matter will be greatly appreciated.

Dr. Brown did not reply. The PHS files contain a draft of a two-page letter dated December 7, 1966, from Brown to Buxtun asserting the value of the study and stating that "All persons in the study have been volunteers and completely free to leave the study at any time. . . . . Through the years all types of [illegible] syphilis therapy have been received by participants in the study, heavy metals in earlier years and penicillin or other antibiotics in later years." However, Brown evidently had second thoughts and the letter was never sent.

Instead, a copy of Buxtun's letter in the PHS files contains Dr. Brown's handwritten notation of March 30, 1967:

> Conference held with Mr. Buxtun. Those present Dr. John Cutler, Dr. James Sencer, Mr. Wm. Waters, Mr. Arthur C___. This matter was discussed in much detail & Mr. Buxtun's specific questions were taken into consideration.

This conference was held in Atlanta at the Centers for Disease Control. Judging from his testimony in 1973 in a Senate hearing on the Study, Buxtun had felt that the March 1967 conference was an exercise in bureaucratic reaction to criticism and he half expected to be fired as a troublemaker. But nothing happened in the months following the conference, and later that year Buxtun resigned on his own initiative from the PHS and entered law school. However, he did not forget about the Study. In November 1968, as a private citizen, Buxtun wrote Dr. Brown again:

> When we discussed the matter in Atlanta, I told you that I had grave moral doubts as to the propriety of this study. While I could see the justification and propriety of the study at its inception, and even up to the time of the widespread use of penicillin, I could not condone the continuation of this study up to the present day. While I must grant the danger of treating aged syphilitics, and while I am sure medical science has benefitted by the study, I still must advocate the following points:
>
> 1.) The group is 100% negro. This in itself is political dynamite and subject to wild journalistic misinterpretation. It also follows the thinking of negro militants that negros have long been used for "medical

experiments" and "teaching cases" in the emergency wards of county hospitals.

2.) The group is not composed of "volunteers with medical motives". They are largely uneducated, unsophisticated, and quite ignorant of the effects of untreated syphilis.

3.) Today it would be morally unethical to begin such a study with such a group. Probably not even the suasion of belonging to the "Nurse Rivers Burial Society" would be sufficient inducement.

I earnestly hope that you will inform me that the study group has been, or soon will be, treated.

Attached to the copy of this letter in the PHS files is a December 16, 1968, handwritten memo by Dr. Brown:

The Tuskegee study was discussed with Dr. Sencer this date. He advised we assemble a small group of physicians to review the objectives and findings and give advice as to where we should go from here. The questions to consider are should the study be continued or not, should the patients be treated & if so what schedule of therapy.

Dr. Sencer advised that after the committee is selected and planning underway that we then write Mr. Buxtun to the effect that there are differences of opinion among the medical profession as whether or not the study members should be treated.

As previously mentioned, this led to the February 1969 ad hoc committee meeting in Atlanta. Some changes were made, but the Study continued, and the public was still unaware of it.

In early 1972 Buxtun told a San Francisco Associated Press reporter about the Study. The AP managers assigned the story to Jean Heller, an investigative reporter based in Washington, D.C. Heller then researched and wrote the story that got my attention on the plane ride in July and that brought Charlie Pollard into my office a few days later. Mr. Pollard learned about the story not from the national media but because a Montgomery reporter, following up on the wire service coverage, found Mr. Pollard's name and tracked him down and interviewed him. Heller subsequently came to Tuskegee and interviewed Mr. Pollard and she subsequently interviewed me, as his attorney, and others in Macon County.

The story was a major news event in Alabama in 1972 and it naturally invited comparisons with all the other racially discriminatory practices which the State of Alabama has unfortunately but deservedly been identified with over the years. Alabama is my home and is a great state, but we are still working hard to overcome the sins of the past.

The Tuskegee Study also invited comparisons with other notorious cases of human medical experimentation. I will discuss some of these in Chapter 10, but the timing of the public exposure of the Study allowed it to become a focus of hearings of a U.S. Senate subcommittee on health chaired by Senator Edward Kennedy. Those hearings covered other topics such as sterilization and shock therapy, but the Tuskegee Study was a centerpiece of the more than two months of hearings in early 1973. Buxtun testified at those hearings, as did I, Mr. Pollard, and Mr. Lester Scott, another Study participant.

I met Peter Buxtun for the first time at the Kennedy hearings. He gave me the impression that he was a very sincere and dedicated person. He was what is now commonly called a "whistleblower." Frankly, if he had not blown the whistle on the Tuskegee Study, it conceivably could still be going on, because several participants have defied the odds and at this writing are still very much alive. We will hear more from them in the chapter about President Clinton's apology.

Incidentally, Heller is now employed with the St. Petersburg, Florida, *Times*. Last year she came back to Tuskegee around the time of the Presidential apology and wrote a follow-up to her dramatic series of articles more than twenty years ago.

6

The Lawsuit

I have been involved with the Tuskegee Syphilis Study since July 27, 1972, when Mr. Charlie Pollard came into my office and asked me if I read the newspaper about the men who were involved in the syphilis tests for "bad blood." He said he was one of the men. He related that a few days before, he was at a stockyard in Montgomery and a newspaper woman found him and questioned him about the Tuskegee testing program, and asked him if he knew Nurse Eunice Rivers. The reporter engaged him in a conversation about his involvement in a health program since back in the thirties. During our conference, Mr. Pollard related in detail his involvement in the experiment. As a result of our discussion, I agreed to represent Mr. Pollard in a lawsuit against the government and others who were legally responsible for operating and maintaining the experiment.

Mr. Pollard's statement confirmed the story I had read while flying from Washington, D.C., to Montgomery a few days earlier. As we saw in the previous chapter, that wire service article by Jean Heller was the first public exposure of the Tuskegee Syphilis Study, although as it developed there was considerable documentation of the Study in the medical literature and there were many doctors, health personnel, undertakers, white employers, college administrators, and draft board members in the Macon County area who had knowledge if not complete understanding of the Study.

When Mr. Pollard came into my office on July 27, 1972, my life was already quite busy. I had many civil rights cases pending in addition to my general practice of law; I was minister of a church; Bernice and I had four small children; I was trying to be a good husband; and I was in the middle of a legislative term, in which I served as one of the first two African Americans elected since Reconstruction to the Alabama House of Representatives.

My legislative service was complicated by the fact that voting rights litigation, which I had been involved in myself, led to a judicial decree that Alabama's unfair state electoral districts would be replaced by single-member districts based on an equal apportionment of the population. Under the old system, which had been in force since the 1901 Alabama Constitution effectively disfranchised African Americans, legislators were elected to the House of Representatives from multi-member districts and the representation was not proportional to the population. This allowed the big planters from the small predominantly African American rural counties to dominate the political process since they had as much power as the representatives from the large urban counties but were accountable mainly to themselves and their cronies. In 1965, African Americans obtained the right to vote, and we had a majority in the district encompassing Macon, Bullock, and Barbour counties. In 1970 I was elected, along with Thomas Reed, the other African American serving in the State Legislature.

I could tell many stories about this period and I did in my first book, *Bus Ride to Justice.* These were very interesting years in Alabama, to put it mildly. In any event, in 1974 there would no longer be two House seats from the district of Macon, Barbour, and Bullock counties. This meant a vigorous campaign against Thomas Reed in the spring of 1974. My wife, Bernice, had some real strong feelings about my running for re-election. She knew I was more qualified than Thomas Reed, but she believed that he was a better politician. She felt that he would probably win the election and that in reality he was more suited for the political shenanigans that went on in the Legislature. She felt that by the time my term ended, I would have proved to the white community and to all that I was an effective legislator, and that African Americans could serve in the Legislature with distinction.

I would have made my contribution, and then I could return and do my work in the church and the law office.

The Tuskegee Syphilis Experiment was just one pending case at Gray, Seay and Langford, the law firm that I had built, with my partners Solomon Seay and Charles Langford, into the largest African American law firm in Alabama at that time. We had offices in Montgomery and Tuskegee and we had many civil, criminal, and civil rights cases. However, I recognized that the Tuskegee Syphilis Study was one of the largest cases I had. Bernice recognized that, too, and she thought, rather than for me to be involved in politics or trying to do so much in the Legislature, I needed to be devoting my time and effort towards this big and very important case. Bernice kept me focused on this case. She would not let me forget it, nor put it on the back burner. She was determined that I devoted the time and effort to this case, because it could be my biggest case. She was right.

Of course, I thought I should stay in the Legislature. So I made up my mind to run for re-election and, as Bernice predicted, I lost the election to Thomas Reed. This turned out to be one of those cases where pride goeth before a fall, but in this case, at least, the fall was for the best because it allowed me to devote my full attention to the lawsuit that was beginning to gather steam.

Conclusions, 1972–1973

As a result of our initial investigation into the case, we reached the following conclusions:

1. The United States government violated the constitutional rights of the participants in the manner in which the study was conducted.

2. The government knew the participants had syphilis and failed to treat them—even after penicillin became available.

3. The Public Health Service failed to fully disclose to the participants that they had syphilis, that they were participating in a study, and that treatment was available for syphilis.

4. The Public Health Service led the participants to believe that they were being properly treated for whatever diseases they had, when in fact, they were not being meaningfully treated.

5. The Public Health Service failed to obtain the participants' written consents to be a part of the study.

6. The Study was racially motivated and discriminated against African Americans in that no whites were selected to participate in the Study; only those who were poor, uneducated, rural and African-American were recruited.

7. There were no rules and regulations governing the Study.

We believed those were the key issues to be resolved in a lawsuit. Of course, once the lawsuit was filed, we must prove our allegations, and in a case involving as many plaintiffs and defendants and stretching over as long a time span as this one, we knew that would be a Goliath-sized task for our David-sized law firm.

Search for Assistance

The work involved in developing this case was tremendous. I was reminded of advice given me by my law school adviser, Professor Samuel Sonnenfield. He encouraged me to seek assistance of other more experienced lawyers, and be willing to share a fee with them, particularly during the early years of my practice. As I had done with civil rights cases throughout my career, I tried to find someone to assist me in this case.

Finding and obtaining assistance was more difficult than I ever imagined. For almost a year, I telephoned and traveled all over the country, looking for someone to help me with this potentially historic case. I needed help in conducting legal research, drafting pleadings, filing briefs, and financing the case.

With previous civil rights cases, I was usually able to obtain such assistance from the NAACP or the NAACP Legal Defense Fund. But both organizations are non-profit corporations, whose policies did not permit them to assist in fee-generating cases.

It was going to take a substantial amount of money to develop this case. I could not find anyone who was willing to give me assistance in my two areas of need.

With a recommendation from Jack Greenberg, director counsel of the NAACP Legal Defense Fund, I sought out Michael I. Sovern, then dean of

Columbia Law School, and one of his professors, Harold Edgar. They agreed to assist me with legal research.

I still had the responsibility of financing the case. I went to my local banker, James Allan Parker, president of Tuskegee's Alabama Exchange Bank, discussed my problem, and he indicated a willingness to make a loan. It was not a loan on a contingent fee basis. No banker would have done that. I would have to pay the bank regardless of the result of the lawsuit. However, he was willing to wait until there was a resolution of the case before the loan would become due. With these two components in hand, I was now ready to file the lawsuit.

Plaintiffs and Defendants

On July 24, 1973, the lawsuit was filed. Jurisdiction was invoked under (1) the Fourth, Fifth, Eighth, Ninth, Thirteenth and Fourteenth Amendments to the U.S. Constitution; (2) the civil rights laws 42 USC Section 1981, Section 1985(3), and Section 2000(D); (3) the Federal Torts Claims Act, 28 USC 2671; (4) the federal common law, and (5) the Constitution, statutes, and common law of Alabama.

This lawsuit was to redress grievances by damages and injunctive relief in order to secure for the plaintiffs themselves, and the class they represented, protection against continued or future deprivation of their rights by the defendants. The goal was to get the government's full attention. Originally, $1.8 billion in damages was sought for the surviving participants and the heirs of those who had died.

In the complaint as finally amended (on August 1, 1974) we had four categories of plaintiffs:

1. Living syphilitics
2. Living controls
3. Personal representatives of the estates of deceased syphilitics
4. Personal representatives of the estates of deceased controls.

The named plaintiffs included Charlie Pollard, Carter Howard, Herman Shaw, Price Johnson, and others. My law partner, Solomon Seay, Jr., assisted with the case. Cleveland Thornton, a young white lawyer from Barbour County and a member of our firm at the time, also assisted me in this case.

The defendants were the United States of America, Casper Weinberger as Secretary of the Department of Health, Education, and Welfare, Dr. Ira L. Myers, State Health Officer; Dr. John R. Heller, individually; Dr. Sidney Olansky, individually; and others. The defendants were represented by William J. Baxley, then Attorney General of Alabama, James T. Pons, Kenneth Vines, Calvin Pryor, Lawrence Klinger, Herman H. Hamilton, Jr., Champ Lyons, W. Michael Atchinson, and Oakley Melton, Jr.

Over the years, I have been asked why I did not include Nurse Eunice Rivers Laurie and Tuskegee Institute as defendants in this case? Isn't it a fact that each of them played a part and should bear some of the blame in connection with the Tuskegee Syphilis Experiment? Did I fail to add them as defendants because they were black and all of the other defendants were white? Did I fail to add them because all of the plaintiffs were African Americans? Isn't it a fact that if I had named them as defendants it would have adversely affected the allegations that the Tuskegee Syphilis Experiment was racist?

All of these questions are related and are fair questions to be considered.

Nurse Rivers was a lone African American female working on a health program financed by the federal government. She was working directly with white doctors from Washington, D.C. Neither the racial climate nor society's attitudes toward government encouraged her questioning the activities of white government officials. She did not question the fact that the government was financing and supporting the program.

She believed she could help, and at the same time she would be helping the federal government. Miss Rivers was powerless to have either begun, continued, or stopped the program. She worked in an environment where all of her superiors were white, while she worked directly with African American men. Even after penicillin became available, Nurse Rivers had no voice as to whether or not these men would be given penicillin. In 1969, a committee was formed to consider whether or not the program she had worked on for more than three decades—and had been the most constant aspect of for more than three decades—should continue. Nurse Rivers was not invited to participate in that discussion or to be a policy-maker in that decision. She was not even consulted. The white doctors from Washington concluded that the experiment should continue and that the participants still should not be treated for syphilis. The Alabama Department of Public Health, for which she also worked, again under the direction of white male doctors, went along with this program from the beginning to the end.

So you have one lone African American female, who from 1932-1972 was supervised by white doctors from Washington and by the white health officer from Macon County, in a program sponsored by the federal government. It would have been unrealistic for Nurse Rivers to express any views opposing the State of Alabama, the Macon County Health Department, white doctors from Washington, D.C., and the United States government. I felt Nurse Rivers was misled, betrayed, and was also a victim of the Tuskegee Syphilis Study. In preparing the lawsuit, after reviewing the facts and circumstances, I was not going to subject her to being a defendant in the case. She was not the moving force in organizing, maintaining, or perpetuating the experiment. She was nothing more than one of many lower-level government employees who were involved in the Study but not named as defendants.

I did not include Tuskegee Institute as a defendant. In the 1930s, during the Great Depression, Tuskegee Institute was an African American educational institution struggling for its very existence. The federal government came to the institution and requested that some facilities of the college hospital be used for the purpose of examining the participants in a health care program. Tuskegee Institute was being asked to cooperate with the federal government in providing health care for the participants. The cooperation was being sought in a study that began as an outgrowth of the Rosenwald Fund survey in Macon County, which was a project of one of Tuskegee Institute's significant benefactors. As with Nurse Rivers, I felt that it would have been unrealistic to expect Tuskegee Institute to refuse to cooperate with the government. Tuskegee Institute administrators were asked to provide facilities and services; they were never invited to review or set policy. I felt the same about Tuskegee Institute as I did about Nurse Rivers—that the Institute and its officials were misled, betrayed, and taken advantage of as she had been.

Interestingly, President Bill Clinton took this same position twenty-five years later when he said:

> Medical people are supposed to help when we need care, but even once a cure was discovered, they were denied help, and they were lied to by their government. Our government is supposed to protect the rights of its citizens; their rights were trampled upon. Forty years ago, hundreds of men were betrayed, along with their wives and children, along with the community in Macon County, Alabama, the City of Tuskegee, the fine university there, and the larger African American community.

So the President, in his apology to surviving Study participants on May 16, 1997, recognized that Tuskegee Institute, along with these participants, and the whole community were lied to and betrayed by the federal government.

The Allegations

In our complaint, we alleged the following basic facts:

1. The participants were poor, Southern, rural, African Americans, of limited education, who knew nothing of their roles as experimental subjects.

2. The Tuskegee Syphilis Study began in 1932 and was announced by employees of the U. S. Public Health Service as a new health care program beginning in Macon County, Alabama. The notices were circulated throughout the county by mail, at African American schools, and African American churches. Only African Americans were given the notices, and only African American males were subsequently selected to participate in the program. None of the participants in the Study were meaningfully treated for syphilis.

3. The participants were never told that they were being solicited to be used in an experiment.

4. The employees of the government purposely did not inform the participants when they were found to have syphilis, and intentionally with-

held this information from them.

5. The government represented to the participants, or gave the impression by words and actions that they were receiving adequate medical treatment for all of their ailments. Such representations or impressions were false and were known to be false by the government. However, each of the participants reasonably believed such representations and participated in the experiment for over forty years.

6. The participants were never advised that any of them had syphilis, and they were never treated for syphilis.

7. The participants never gave their informed consent to be subjects in any such experiment.

8. No white persons were solicited or used in the Study.

9. Those selected were used in a program of controlled genocide solely because of their race and color in violation of their rights, secured by the Constitution and laws of the State of Alabama.

10. The government exploited the participants in violation of rights guaranteed under the Fifth, Ninth, Thirteenth, and Fourteenth Amendments to the Constitution of the United States, and Article I, Section VI of the Alabama Constitution of 1901. Plaintiffs further alleged that they were injured physically and mentally. They were afflicted with distress, pain, discomfort, and suffering. Some died as a result of participating in the Study.

Theory of the Case

The theory of the case was that the government had breached its duty to the participants in failing to obtain informed consent, inform them of the nature and purposes of the experiment, and inform them of the possible hazards and effects upon the health of the participants which might result from their participation.

The government had a duty to the plaintiffs once penicillin became available to treat those who had syphilis, which it failed to do. The government violated the civil rights of the plaintiffs in that it and state officials acted under color of State law by denying them their constitutional rights of equal protection, of due process, and of privacy. The government was negligent in conducting the Tuskegee Syphilis Experiment without any established protocol for conducting the experiment, thus subjecting the participants to unnecessary risks.

Defendant Dr. R. L. Myers, State Health Officer, filed an answer on September 29, 1973, substantially denying the basic allegations and raising, as a second defense, that there was insufficient information to determine whether or not all of the subjects were African American, poor, and uneducated.

On May 14, 1974, the defendant United States answered the complaint, and alleged as defenses:

1. The action was barred by the statute of limitations.

2. The injuries and damages alleged by the complaint were caused without the fault, carelessness, or negligence on the part of the defendant or any of its agents, servants, or employees acting within the line and scope of their employment.

3. It denied that the injuries and damages to the participants, as alleged in the complaint, were caused by acts of negligence, or carelessness on the part of the government.

The government substantially denied all of the material allegations of the complaint. The United States admitted, however, that the Experiment began in 1932, that the participants were African American and were in the Study; that the Study was conducted by the federal government, and that some participants had died since 1932. It denied that the causes of death were related to the Study. That was the position of the United States of America when the suit was filed in 1973.

Discovery

One major problem in preparing the case for trial was the matter of obtaining discovery. According to the federal rules of civil procedure, after a lawsuit is filed, and prior to trial, a party may obtain any and all information which the other party has that may be relevant to the lawsuit. This is called discovery. We utilized several forms of discovery including depositions, interrogatories, requests for admissions, and requests for production. Interrogatories are written questions which must be answered in writing and sworn to under oath the same as if the answers were given orally in court. Interrogatories were propounded to the known living doctors involved in the Study and proper officials of the Public Health Service and to the government, but many of the answers were inconclusive. The response to the motion to produce documents during the early part of the study was met with a "no records available so far as the government knew."

The plaintiffs then undertook to try and find these records. As a result of our independent efforts, I met Jim Jones, a medical researcher, who had located the early records of the study, from 1931–1939, scattered through some 410 boxes in the National Archives. He literally searched through each individual box and picked out the information that was applicable to the Tuskegee Syphilis Study. Jim Jones's work was significant and made my task less difficult. He later wrote an excellent book about the study entitled *Bad Blood* and is now a professor of history at the University of Houston.

Opening Estates for Deceased Participants

During the course of our litigation, we were confronted with many legal problems. As indicated early during the discovery period, the government did not know and could not locate the early documents that would give us the facts concerning the origin of the Study. There were questions as to whether or not this was an appropriate class action suit. There were serious questions concerning the suit being barred by the statue of limitations. There were major problems of standing—who had the legal right to bring the action on behalf of the deceased participants in the Study.

The original complaint was filed on behalf of the widows and heirs of deceased participants. The defendants raised the issue of standing, saying that under Alabama law, the only person who could sue for a deceased person is the personal representative of the individual estate. That meant, in the cases of participants who had died without wills, it would be necessary to file a petition in the Probate Court of Macon County in each case and have someone appointed personal representative of that persons' estate. Under Alabama law, in addition to filing an application for Letters of Administration, a bond must be filed in an amount twice the value of the estate prior to the Court granting Letters of Administration. The person who petitioned the for the Letters of Administration must be a resident of the State of Alabama. Many of the deceased participants had died outside of Alabama.

This was a serious problem. The Court entered an order stating that the personal representative was the proper party to file a suit on behalf of the deceased participants, and gave us a short period of time in which to have them appointed. This was a difficult task. We needed to have appointed personal representatives for each of the deceased participants. There were 463 deceased participants. Under most circumstances this would have been an impossible task. First, we had to find individuals who were familiar with the deceased participants, for example, wives, children, close relatives, or friends. In instances where we could find none, we asked people we knew if they would serve as personal representatives of the estates of deceased participants. This required tremendous cooperation between people in the community. These men lived in all parts of Macon County. We began to talk with persons throughout the county and lined up persons who signed individual petitions, and had individuals to sign bonds so the administration could be completed.

In addition to the community involvement and finding persons to serve as administrators, we also had to locate persons who would sign bonds on behalf of these petitioners. The Judge of Probate of Macon County, in the final analysis, had to sign the order approving the bonds and appointing a personal representative on each of these estates. How could our Probate Office with its limited resources be able to accomplish such a task? I discussed this entire matter with the Honorable Preston Hornsby, Judge of Probate of Macon County. He knew the families of many of these men. In addition, he was the best politician in the county. Prior to the time he was elected Probate Judge, he was Sheriff of Macon County. In the first major campaign where blacks were able to vote, he openly solicited African-American votes and was elected Sheriff of Macon County. After successfully serving in that capacity, he ran for and became Judge of Probate.

After I discussed this matter with Judge Hornsby, he understood, was sympathetic, and gave whole-hearted support to our efforts. We literally moved a part of the Probate Office out of the Courthouse and into our office where we were able to prepare all of these documents. Within the time frame appointed by the Court and with the assistance of Judge Hornsby, we were able to have personal representatives appointed on the estates of each of the deceased participants. When the complaint was amended and filed on August 1, 1974, we had personal representatives of the estates of deceased syphilitics and personal representatives of deceased controls as plaintiffs in the suit.

What Our Research Proved

The mountain of documents eventually unearthed showed that, unquestionably, government doctors knew from the inception of the Study that the participants believed they were in a treatment program. Along with letters from the project nurse indicating this, they received letters from participants' friends asking to be included in the government treatment program.

What was done to participants in order to secure information about untreated syphilitics? Among the overreaching steps by the United States in the early years were:

1. The United States' doctors wrote and visited every local doctor in the area, gave them a list of patients in the study, syphilitics and controls, and secured their cooperation in the study. This cooperation included not treating anyone for syphilis because it would spoil the data.

2. United States' doctors sent these participant lists to "prominent lay people" (almost certainly white employers) to facilitate follow-up.

3. The doctors sent annual letters to participants telling them the federal doctors were coming again to treat their bad blood, and to find out whether past treatment had improved their condition.

4. Public Health Service personnel stopped participants from receiving treatment from the traveling State public health clinics and at other opportunities for treatment.

5. The Public Health Service wrote, through the Alabama Board of Health, to the local draft boards in 1941 to make sure that these men were not called for wartime physicals which would disclose syphilis and make treatment mandatory. Initially, the persons thus deprived included not only the original syphilitics, but also controls who had developed syphilis in the

intervening years and had received no treatment for it. No effort was made to assure that these persons' wives and children had been treated.

6. The doctors and nurse handed out substantial quantities of painkillers such as aspirin and tonics, as well as some codeine, as an inducement to stay in the program, knowing the participants thought it was curative treatment for their ills.

7. The doctors did all this while their own medical records and reports they published were demonstrating unequivocally that the syphilitics were dying faster, and experiencing higher rates of heart morbidity than were the controls. That point was clear to the doctors from the very beginning, and it was duly monitored by articles that plotted participants' "death curves." Notwithstanding their own knowledge of the heightened death curve of the non-treated syphilitics, the deliberate and affirmative program of non-treatment was continued. Moreover, an intentional decision was made not to monitor the patients for a variety of other ailments, including, most tragically, neurosyphilis.

In summary, from 1933 on, the Study strayed far from its original short-term goals. Unlike the initial one-shot survey, the long-term research design was not evaluated carefully, and the rights of the humans involved were completely submerged to the researchers' desires to get just a little more return on their invested capital. This was the progression: the 1932 survey data, coming from syphilitics only, showed that untreated syphilitics had severe health problems, and much more complex ones than had been expected. That finding raised this question: How much damage was syphilitic in origin, and how much was the product of adverse environment? Further, the 1932–33 findings of massive heart abnormalities could be undercut if heart specialists challenged the diagnostic techniques used. To preclude challenge to the Study's conclusions on either ground, the solution was to select a group of controls from the surveyed non-positive-Wassermann Negroes, and follow both groups for a while in order to "bring the material to autopsy." The doctors would confirm the initial 1932 diagnoses, reject the environmental hypothesis, and additionally measure interim syphilitic damage.

This was the long-term study plan and its effectuation, as unconscionable then as now. The Tuskegee experiment was not done with therapeutic hopes. There is not the slightest question but that the doctors who established and ran this program believed, based upon the careful Rosenwald records, that the then current medications posed trivial risks compared to the consequences of untreated syphilis. CDC's effort in 1972 to portray this study in its early years as potentially beneficial given the perceived dangers of mercury and arsenicals is inaccurate. Exactly the opposite is true. The doctors were so sure that untreated syphilis was a deadly serious problem, and that treatment was efficacious, that they wanted to prove it beyond question by control group comparisons and autopsies that would rule out any other possible explanation of data. Based on the documents, this process permitting these participants to suffer and die, seems never to have concerned the doctors in the least. The program doctors simply failed to think of the patients, their wives, or their children as human beings. This program of non-treatment then lasted forty years.

As far as later doctors were concerned, in relation to this group, penicillin's discovery was a regrettable event, worrisome lest it pollute the sample. In their 1955 article, "Untreated Syphilis in the Male Negro," Schuman, et al., analyzed participants' treatment status. The authors note that eight of the men had received adequate penicillin treatment by 1951 (with seroreversal in three cases), and mention no ensuing complications. They further note that the surviving syphilitic group is now 70 percent untreated, 22.5 percent inadequately treated, and 7.5 percent adequately treated. But they argue that those patients who have had some treatment should be followed still:

> [In] 1952 they are veterans of an aggregate of 5494.5 man-years of untreated disease, in comparison to only 28.5 man-years of adequately treated disease.
>
> Since the man-years of adequately treated disease represents such a small part of the total years of observation, and in most patients the treatment was administered many years after the date of the initial infection, it is felt that the antibiotic era has not defeated the purpose

of the study."

The authors' perception of the significance of penicillin in terms of whether it spoiled the research ought to be juxtaposed against their other findings:

> [T]he single most striking feature distinguishing the syphilitic group from the nonsyphilitic is that the death rate is higher among the syphilitic group. Exactly how and why more of the syphilitic group has died is not clearly discernible, but the penalty which the syphilitic patients have paid in terms of life expectancy is well-documented.

How could this disregard of human safety and life capacity have been allowed to continue? By the 1950s, a patient discovered to have latent syphilis would have been treated with antibiotics by almost every doctor in the United States, using bismuth if necessary to control adverse reactions, reactions that can occur only if the treponemes are alive and potentially dangerous.

So far as can be ascertained from the documents, no course of treatment was formally or informally considered for these African Americans until a young Public Health Service worker began complaining in 1966. Literally, not one single piece of paper out of the thousands of pages discussing every aspect of the study discusses whether treatment ought to be given. The documents reveal that the doctors believed in 1952 that a twenty-year investment should not go to waste, that this was the last opportunity to study untreated syphilis, and incredibly, that having shortened the lives of so many, they should press on with the work even though it might mean further premature deaths and disability. Even in 1969, treatment was rejected by a committee for reasons which patently included the desire to continue the Study and obtain just a little more information from the group. Compelling evidence that the 1969 determination was not made on the basis of the patients' medical needs is that each and every one of these very same participants was uniformly urged to get treated in 1972 after the Study was exposed.

The new doctors, in the 1960s, worked and acted in an era where the requirement of informed consent for experiments was formal and unambiguous. They knew perfectly well they did not have consent, and that these men were "at risk," albeit the risk may have been lower for the participants whose syphilis was still latent after thirty years of non-treatment. Moreover, statistics hide individual cases. One terribly potent indictment is that the subjects, ever since 1932, would have nothing to do with spinal taps. Those first taps, Vonderlehr's Golden Needle treatment, performed without anesthetics, were exceptionally painful. The Study's internal documents often treat the fearful reactions to this pain as proof of some rural superstitions of the participants.

Our investigation, however, led us to believe, that Dr. Vonderlehr did the taps poorly, a view shared by Nurse Rivers. Dr. Vonderlehr was tired, overworked, and very anxious because he had to get all the taps done before word of what was happening spread among the participants. After the initial taps, most of the participants made it very clear they would never submit to such a procedure again, so the PHS officials early abandoned any hope of making spinal taps a routine part of the annual checkup and the five-year surveys, fearing the Study would collapse. The doctors acknowledged they could not use the only effective diagnostic procedure available to test the presence of one of the more serious complications of syphilis. Yet the doctors knew the threat of neurosyphilis was real: 23 percent of the participants had it in 1932 when the first survey was done. Of the first participants examined once the Study ended, 16 percent had neurosyphilis.

Finally, doctors who knew penicillin was a remedy for syphilis permitted the Study to proceed because of apparent statistical safety based on the controls' death rates. The use of the controls' life-expectancy as the test of safety was questionable. It assumed the comparability of the two groups except for syphilis, an assumption later doctors expressly made. However, the survey techniques utilized by Vonderlehr to get his initial sample were weighted to pick up syphilitic persons of greater than average hardiness, in that they had survived syphilis thus far and were out doing heavy work. Field hands and manual workers were sought out by Vonderlehr so that he would not have to waste his Wassermann tests on women.

The later doctors assumed comparability because they had never read the file on how the syphilitics were selected. They made the mistake of relying on their predecessors' writings, including its reports of the participants volunteering in droves at churches and schools. But the doctors stopped working at churches in January 1933, because for every man presenting himself, three women would seek testing. If the doctors refused to treat women, the men refused to cooperate because they thought the doctors were from the Army. So the doctors went to the saw mills, the Public Works employment centers, and into the fields with Keidel tubes. The Wassermann positive rates with Keidel tubes were well below those at the churches, indicating that those syphilitics capable of doing heavy work were more than usually sturdy. It should have been no surprise, given the relative hardiness required to get into the two sample populations, that syphilitics in later years might even be doing better than controls.

Nothing the doctors might have learned about untreated syphilis could possibly justify this calculated mistreatment of a group of United States citizens. An added dimension of this tragedy is that the study was poorly done in scientific terms. Nearly all these patients were given some treatment with arsenicals or mercury, and often with both, in the course of the initial 1932–33 survey. The amount was believed too small to have much effect on the disease, but it ruined the study as one of untreated syphilis. The doctors botched the sample doing the short-term study, securing it by going through the motions of treatment, before a long-term study was even contemplated. Rather than call it quits, the doctors falsified the sample selection procedure in their initial papers by arbitrarily defining the little treatment as no treatment at all. Although it baffled later doctors how so many patients had gotten some, albeit obviously inadequate, treatment, no one had read the files. The files were found in the National Archives, meaning that an on-going medical experiment was conducted with no one involved even knowing where the papers pertinent to its initial design and early years were kept.

The Settlement

The government did not begin to discuss the possibility of settlement until after we obtained much of the information detailed in the earlier chapters of this book and made it known by appropriate court pleadings and briefs.

Ultimately, we were successful in getting financial compensation for each of the living participants and the heirs of deceased participants in the Tuskegee Syphilis Study. In addition, the government was ordered to continue its health care program for the living participants and widows and children of any participants who tested positively for syphilis.

While the final $10 million settlement was not what I had hoped to receive for my clients, considering all of the facts and circumstances, it was in my opinion fair and reasonable. This study started in 1932. There were a multiplicity of legal problems that would have to be resolved if there had been a trial. If this case were discovered today under the same facts and circumstances, the value of the case would be substantially higher. When the proceeds from the settlement were paid into court, the funds were placed in an interest-bearing account. It took a number of years to locate all the participants, and after the recipients had received the principal amount there was accumulated interest to disburse. Thus, we had to verify again whether the participants were living or dead, and if dead, whether there were living heirs, and in all cases we had to find current addresses. This case is still pending.

The settlement was divided into four categories:

(1) Living syphilitics received $37,500.

(2) Heirs of deceased syphilitics received $15,000.

(3) Living controls received $16,000.

(4) Heirs of deceased controls received $5,000.

The persons who suffered most and whose lives were at risk were the syphilitics. Though many received some incidental or even accidental treatment over the years, they were never treated for syphilis during the experiment, not even after penicillin became available. The controls did not have syphilis. Neither they nor their wives and children were at risk. That is why there was a difference in the amounts for the syphilitics and the controls.

When the proceeds from the settlement were paid into court, the funds were placed into an interest-bearing account. The next task was to locate the living participants and the heirs of the deceased participants. This was a major task and it took years to accomplish. Originally, we did not know who the heirs of the deceased participants were, so we had to find them. When we began to find heirs and people realized there was money involved, it became necessary to have hearings to determine who were the legitimate heirs. The principal amount of funds were finally completely distributed in 1992, except for interest payments. Then, the process started all over again to distribute the interest payments. Many who were paid principal amounts had died and we had to locate their heirs. However, more than six thousand persons have received compensation. We are still looking for some heirs to distribute interest money.

When it became generally known that money was available, some men and women claimed falsely to have been in the Experiment. In instances where participants were deceased, some falsely claimed to be heirs. As a result, during the time when claims were being litigated, the court held hearings on conflicting claims dealing with heirs.

In addition to the financial settlements, the government was ordered to continue providing other benefits including free health care for living participants and to the families of syphilitic participants, as well as free burial expenses for participants based on the cost of living index at the time of their deaths.

7

An Abrupt End to the Study

While we were developing the lawsuit in late 1972 and early 1973, the Study itself was finally getting the public spotlight that it had managed to avoid for forty years. Jean Heller's first news report was published on July 25, 1972. The very next day, government spokesmen, including some from PHS itself, began condemning the Study.

The various responses generally took the form of admitting that the Study had been wrong, but that it had begun in an era when both medical and social conditions were very different. Outside agencies and institutions which had been involved tried to shift the responsibility solely to the PHS. Despite the fact that in 1969 State Health Officer Dr. Ira Myers had approved continuing the Study under the auspices of the Macon County Health Department, he now said Alabama health personnel had helped PHS only in "evaluation." Macon County private physicians, who had agreed in 1969 that the surviving syphilitics would not be treated, now said they did not know that treatment was being withheld. The Tuskegee Veterans Administration Hospital denied any direct involvement. Tuskegee Institute issued a statement that its staff and facilities had been used in the 1930s as a part of a large-scale anti-syphilis effort but that the Study had been shifted to the local health department in the 1940s.

The federal government, meanwhile, quickly condemned the Study and launched an investigation. By this time, the Study was operating under the Centers for Disease Control in Atlanta, under the larger umbrella of the U.S. Department of Health, Education, and Welfare. Assistant Secretary of HEW was Dr. Merlin K. Duval, into whose lap the Study fell. He declared he was "horrified" by the Study and on August 24, 1972, announced that an investigation would be conducted by the Tuskegee Syphilis Study Ad Hoc Panel. Nine non-PHS employees, five of them African American, were named to the panel under the chairmanship of Dillard University President Broadus Nathaniel Butler, a nationally prominent African American educator.

Dr. Butler's group was given three charges:

> I. Determine whether the study was justified in 1932 and whether it should have been continued when penicillin became generally available.

> II. Recommend whether the study should be continued at this point in time, and if not, how it should be terminated in a way consistent with the rights and health needs of its remaining participants.

> III. Determine whether existing policies to protect the rights of patients participating in health research conducted or supported by the Department of Health, Education, and Welfare are adequate and effective and to recommend improvements in these policies if needed.

The Ad Hoc Panel wasted little time in presenting its initial recommendations. On October 25, 1972, temporarily bypassing charges I and III, the Panel recommended the immediate termination of the Tuskegee Syphilis Study and the provision of any medical care the surviving participants might need.

On November 16, 1972, HEW Assistant Secretary Duval issued an administrative order ending the Study.

The Panel's work on the other charges continued through April 1973, when it issued a final report declaring that even though there may have been some scientific reason to conduct a brief study in 1932, the overall Study was ethically unjustified even from the beginning; that the withholding of penicillin beginning in the 1940s was especially wrong; and that existing HEW/PHS safeguards were insufficient to protect subjects from such studies.

In early 1973, the specialists appointed by the Ad Hoc Panel to look into methods of providing medical care to the survivors agreed that Tuskegee Institute's Andrew Memorial Hospital was the best facility to provide this care, and negotiations began with the hospital concerning funding and the type and duration of the care to be provided.

After the Experiment became generally known, the Tuskegee Administrative Hoc Advisory Panel was appointed. This Panel, among other things recommended whether the Experiment should end. They invited Mr. Charlie Pollard to appear before them. He accepted provided his counsel could accompany him. They did not want him to attend with counsel. I wrote requesting to appear before the Panel but was denied the privilege of appearing. Therefore, the Ad Hoc Panel joined the organizers of the Study in failing to include the participants in deciding their own fate.

U.S. Senate Hearings

While the Ad Hoc Panel was doing its work and my law firm was preparing for a possible lawsuit, Senator Edward Kennedy of Massachusetts held hearings on human experimentation. Senator Kennedy was chairman of the Senate Subcommittee on Health. I was invited on two separate occasions to bring participants to Washington to testify about their experiences. I took four participants—Charlie Pollard, Herman Shaw, Carter Howard, and Lester Scott—to Washington and they testified. Mr. Pollard stated: "I was going to school in 1932 when they came around and gave me a blood test. They said I had bad blood . . . and they was working on it." Mr. Scott, who was recruited from his farm in 1932, stated: "I thought I was getting shots for bad blood." Asked by Senator Kennedy what he thought of the study now that he knew its real purpose, Scott said: "I don't think much of it. They were just using us for something else—for an experiment. If they had told me, I would have gone to a family doctor and got treated." As a result of their testimony, Congress passed legislation which prohibits this kind of experimentation from occurring again.

State of Alabama Response

Governor George Wallace declared soon after the Study was revealed that an investigation would be held to determine if any Alabama laws had been broken. A number of state health laws did seem to have been violated, but no legal action was ever taken by the state other than to have state attorneys defend the Alabama health officials we ultimately named as defendants in the lawsuit. However, a bill to pay the participants or their heirs twenty-five thousand dollars each was introduced in Congress by Alabama Senators John Sparkman and Jim Allen. No action was taken on the bill.

8

Aftermath

The Tuskegee Syphilis Study ended in 1972, and the lawsuit resulting from it was settled in 1975. Yet almost a quarter-century later, the Study continues to make news and stimulate the public interest. In examining the twenty-five years that have passed since the Study was exposed and the lawsuit filed, some of the key areas to consider include:

1. Its impact on standards and safeguards for medical and scientific research.

2. Its racial dimensions and role in the human rights movement.

3. The importance of the case to the participants; notwithstanding the attention given to the Tuskegee Syphilis Study, little consideration has been given to the participants' own ideas or desires about long-term responses.

4. The worldwide journalistic, historical, and artistic interpretation the Study has received.

Standards Resulting from the Study

Today, in order for the government, or anyone else, to conduct such studies, there must be proper protocol. There must be informed consent. The persons must know they are involved in a study, and proper safeguards must be in place so that their individual rights are protected.

The case reaffirmed the principle that prior informed consent should be obtained from individuals before they are allowed to participate in human experimentations. As a result of this, the government has re-evaluated the use of human beings and experiments and has set minimum standards in order to conduct human experimentations.

Racial and Ethnic Dimensions

Earlier, I observed that the only participants in the Study were African-American and that in my opinion, this Study would never have happened to white participants.

I saw the Experiment as a case of racial discrimination and in that sense it became very personal to me, for I had dedicated my legal career to challenging the Jim Crow segregation under which the participants and I were born and lived. The Study was as racist as segregation in schools, which I fought and won. It was just as racist as segregation in juries, which I fought and won. It was just as racist as segregation in the Alabama farm programs, in housing, public accommodations, and in the political process, all of which I fought and won. Twenty-five years later, President Clinton agreed with me. He said: "To our African American citizens, I am sorry that your federal government orchestrated a study so clearly racist." The Study was conducted solely with blacks when there were also whites in the community who had syphilis, making this case a great opportunity to continue to destroy segregation and discrimination in another area, the health care field.

The Participants

The lawsuit was very important to the persons involved in it, not only for the financial settlement, the medical care, and the burial expenses which they received, but for safeguards that were written so that other persons would not become victims of similar studies.

The significance of this case was that the United States of America, in effect, admitted to wrongdoing and was willing to compensate the aggrieved parties. This case also demonstrated that the judicial process is a viable means of rectifying wrongs perpetrated against the citizens of this country regardless of their race or economic status.

One important point which has been mentioned earlier but cannot be overemphasized is that the syphilitic participants in the study were selected because they had the disease for at least two to five years. Thus, they were in the secondary stage of the disease and were not contagious to others. The lack of public awareness on this point is, I am sure, behind the question I sometimes asked about how the surviving men were received in their communities after it was known that they were participants in the Study, and some of them had syphilis. Few adverse reactions were reported to me. Macon County has a small population of about 2,000, so with over 623 men being involved in the Experiment, many of the participants were related by blood or marriage to people throughout the County. Other participants were leaders in the community, church, and civic and social life. So the men themselves were generally accepted without stigma attached to their having been involved in the Experiment.

Another question that is asked is how the wives reacted when they found out that their husbands were involved in the Experiment, especially the syphilitics who had not been treated. Unfortunately, all of the wives of the current living participants, except one, are deceased. I posed this question to the husbands, who said their wives took the position that their husbands were the same individuals as before they received this knowledge; it had no adverse affect upon them. When you have been married to a person over the years, and you find out something, and the party still acts the same as they have acted in the past, why should there be any real difference in that relationship? They did not permit the disclosure of this information to affect that relationship.

This book is being published in 1998, so at this time it has been sixty-six years since the Study began. Almost all of the participants—both syphilitics and controls—are deceased. However, seven of the men are still living and several are in remarkably good health for their ages.

It would be good to meet them:

• MR. CHARLIE POLLARD is the original and the lead plaintiff in the lawsuit. He and his parents, unlike most participants, were large landowners in the Notasulga area since before the turn of the century. He and his father farmed cattle, corn, cotton, and other crops, and probably had the first mechanical cotton picker in Macon County, certainly the first owned by African Americans. So, he was well respected. Mr. Pollard was born

April 13, 1906, in Macon County. He was married to Louisa Woods for 54 years and has one daughter, Ralphine Harper. He was educated at the Shiloh School, which at that time only went through the seventh grade and for only seven months a year. He has remained a life-long resident of Notasulga and was one of the community leaders who worked for civil rights and cooperated with Dr. C. G. Gomillion in helping to get African Americans registered to vote and elected to public office. He is also a member of Shiloh Missionary Baptist Church, where he was recruited to be a Study participant by Nurse Eunice Rivers and Dr. Murray D. Smith.

• MR. HERMAN SHAW was born May 18, 1902, in Tallapoosa County, just across the line from Macon County. His mother died and his father moved to Plano, Texas, in 1909 where he was educated in the public schools. In 1923, he studied Latin, Algebra, and Greek, and was an excellent student. Had Mr. Shaw had the opportunity to go to college, he would have excelled. He was married to Fannie Mae Greathouse for sixty-two years. The Shaws educated their children well. Herman Shaw, Jr., received a B.S. degree from Alabama A&M and a Master's from North Carolina A&T and became a principal in Etowah County. Mr. Shaw's daughter, Mary Mullins, is a graduate of Tennessee A&I University and worked as a professional and legal secretary in Tuskegee. He has six grandchildren and one great-grandchild. For forty-four years Mr. Shaw worked at the Tallassee Mill in Tallassee, Alabama. The proud owner of a 1941 International tractor which is still in good condition, he still operates his farm and only recently sold his livestock. He has driven Buicks since 1914 and at age ninety-five is still driving his 1989 Park Avenue. He belongs to the New Adka Baptist Church. In recent years, he has served as spokesman for the participants.

• MR. CARTER HOWARD was born February 18, 1904, in Macon County. He grew up in the Oak Grove Community and went to a one-room school where he completed the fifth grade. He is a bachelor who made his living as a farmer and carpenter. He received a pacemaker recently and is in marginal health. Hunting has been one of his hobbies. He is a member of Mt. Ester A.M.E. Zion Church.

• MR. FRED SIMMONS, according to the government's records, was born April 6, 1897, in Macon County, but his children say he say he is actually close to one hundred and ten years of age. He was married to Margaret Tolbert Simmons and they had twenty-one children of which seven are still living. He has many grandchildren and great-grandchildren. He went to the New Hope School, but received very little education, stopping in the second or third grade. He is a member of Mt. Pleasant Baptist Church. His work experience includes plowing, pulpwooding, public work on the railroad, and a little farming.

• MR. ERNEST HENDON was born February 12, 1907, in Macon County. He is single. He attended the Macon County Training School, finishing the twelfth grade. He has about six or seven nieces and nephews. He is a member of Sweet Pilgrim Baptist Church. He has been a farmer most of his life and worked in Cleveland, Ohio, for a chemical company for about twenty-eight years. He is in good health.

• MR. FREDERICK MOSS was born December 12, 1910, in Lee County, Alabama. He has been married since 1936 to his wife, Beatrice, from Macon County. He worked at the shell plant in Macon County and washed cars. He was a member of Mt. Zion Baptist Church in Loachapoka and sang in the choir. Poor health in recent years forced him to move into a nursing home, first in Etowah County and, at this writing, in Tuskegee.

• MR. GEORGE KEY was born April 9, 1907, in Macon County. He was married for sixty years to his wife, Lucille, until her death in 1990. He worked on farms, in public work, and on construction jobs. He now lives in Massachusetts.

You have met the living participants. Much has been written about the Tuskegee Syphilis Study and about the participants. From the beginning of the Study until the end, and evening during the aftermath, very little consideration has been given to them as individuals and what they want as the legacy of the Study.

In recent years the living participants have received a modest amount of public attention resulting from their roles in the Experiment. On February 6, 1997, I was invited to speak at Booker T. Washington High School in Tuskegee, Alabama, during Black History Month. I invited Mr. Charlie Pollard as my guest and introduced him to a warm ovation. When the

Macon County Democratic Club and the Macon County Democratic Executive Committee held their biannual banquet in 1992, it honored all persons who were plaintiffs in civil rights cases in Macon County, including the participants in the Tuskegee Syphilis Experiment. Mr. Herman Shaw and Mr. Charlie Pollard were among those who attended. In March 1998, the men were again honored by the Macon County Democratic Executive Committee and given a modest cash award. On April 4, 1998, in Atlanta, Georgia, the Women of SCLC (Southern Christian Leadership Conference) awarded the men its Drum Major for Justice Award; former Ambassador Andrew Young and Secretary of Transportation Rodney Slater were given a similar award at the program.

Miss Evers' Boys

However, the most significant attention to the participants and to the Study in recent years has come through the play and subsequent HBO movie *Miss Evers' Boys*. These were dramatizations of the Study that focused in large measure on the role of the woman who worked with the participants for practically its entire duration.

The play has been performed in Atlanta, Georgia, at the Alliance Theater and in Montgomery, Alabama, at the Alabama Shakespeare Festival, and several other cities.

It is an understatement that the surviving participants did not like the HBO movie. I was extremely upset by this movie, too. The play was not as objectionable, but the movie version upset those of us in Macon County so much that, as we shall see in the next chapter, it played a role in securing a Presidential apology for the Study.

Immediately after I saw *Miss Evers' Boys,* I called my secretary and requested that she arrange a meeting with the participants for Monday, February 24, in my office so that they could view a tape of the movie. Mr. Charlie Pollard, Mr. Herman Shaw, Mr. Fred Simmons, and Mr. Carter Howard responded. After viewing the movie they were mad, hurt, and felt they had really been taken advantage of once again. They wanted me to do something so that the nation would know the movie was inaccurate. I told them I would. This is the same thing I told Mr. Pollard twenty-five years earlier, when he initially came in my office in July of 1972.

At the press conference called by the participants and held April 8, 1997, at the Shiloh Missionary Baptist Church, I stated in detail the participants' objections to *Miss Evers' Boys*. The points I outlined include:

1. The film did not accurately portray the participants or the events and circumstances of the Study as the men had participated in it.

2. The movie opened by stating that the men were solicited to participate in a program for the treatment of syphilis and that they were treated for a period of time before funding became unavailable. The fact is, the participants were never meaningfully treated for syphilis from the beginning of the Study to the end.

3. The film portrayed a Dr. Brady, an African American physician, as the supervisor of the Study and as Nurse Evers's immediate supervisor. There was no such African American who generally supervised Nurse Rivers nor the Study. All the supervisors were whites. The persons who conceived and sold the Study to the Public Health Service for funding were all whites. The doctors who came to Macon County and examined the participants were all whites. The white Macon County health officer, Dr. Murray D. Smith, accompanied Nurse Rivers when she was recruiting participants for the Study.

4. Thus, the entire film shifts the responsibility for the Study from the federal government to an African American doctor and an African American nurse. This Study was conceived, financed, executed, and administered by the federal government. The African American medical professionals who participated in it were victims as were the 623 African American participants.

5. The film conspicuously omits the role that the State of Alabama, through its health agencies, played in the Study. The Alabama Health Department cooperated with the federal government in continuing not to treat the participants after penicillin became available, notwithstanding that Alabama laws required such treatment.

6. The film used four characters who were referred to as "Miss Evers' boys" to represent all the 623 men in the Study. These men were basically shown as musicians and dancers. That is not accurate. The men who par-

ticipated in the Study, for the most part, were hard-working, reputable persons in their communities. The depiction of them as dancers and "shuffling sams" who lived a carefree existence of drinking, dancing, singing, and cutting up, is a great misrepresentation of the way people had to work in rural Macon County in the 1930s and 1940s just to make a simple living. Viewers of the film would think that these four men were typical not only of the other 619 men in the Study but also of other African Americans who lived in Macon County at that time and even now. This is a tremendous insult and a gross misrepresentation.

7. The film inaccurately represented the character of Nurse Eunice Rivers. Each of the participants, after reviewing the film, stated that Nurse Rivers was always professional and courteous to them. She did not accompany them to juke joints. The participants did not dance, play music, and entertain people at juke joints with Nurse Rivers. There is nothing in the historical account and nothing that these men remember observing about Nurse Rivers which would indicate that she had a love affair with one or more of the participants as was set forth in the film. Nurse Rivers did not give penicillin to one participant and withhold it from all the others.

The participants and I were not the only ones who were troubled by the film. Within a few days after the showing of *Miss Evers' Boys,* I received telephone calls from several persons around the country who were upset over the movie and who offered their assistance in getting the truth to the media.

The interesting thing about Miss Eunice Rivers is that when you asked any of the participants in the experiment, including those seven who are still alive, what they thought about her, the response was unanimous. Every one of them believed that she was a fine person, she was a professional, and she treated them fairly. As a matter of fact, Charlie Pollard, Herman Shaw, Fred Simmons, and Carter Howard, after viewing *Miss Evers' Boys,* were astonished, because they felt Miss Rivers was improperly projected in that movie. They did not believe that she treated any one of the participants better than the others, or that she had a love affair with one of them, or that she took them to night clubs, danced, and drank corn liquor with them.

Very few African Americans at that time had a college education. Eunice Rivers was one of them. She finished Tuskegee Institute (now Tuskegee University) and was a certified nurse. In the late 1920s Nurse Rivers had been a demonstration agent with a mobile school that taught hygiene and health throughout the rural areas. This was probably the only health service that many African-Americans received in Macon County at that time. Then she was a night nursing supervisor in the Andrew Memorial Hospital at Tuskegee Institute. And then she became the project nurse for a new health program that the United States government was proposing to study the effects of untreated syphilis on African Americans.

It is interesting to note how the federal government felt about Nurse Rivers. Over her thirty-plus year career with the Public Health Service, she received many awards, including the Oveta Culp Hobby Award, which was the highest award given by the PHS to its staff members and was presented to her in a ceremony in Washington, D.C., in 1958.

Nurse Rivers devoted substantially all of her life to working with the Study participants over a forty-year period. The tragedy and the unfortunate part of it all is that she was so wrongfully, and improperly portrayed in *Miss Evers' Boys*.

The Trees Don't Bleed In Tuskegee

I have been critical of the movie *Miss Evers' Boys* because it is not factual, and it does not accurately portray the roles that nurse Rivers or the participants played in the Study. There is a proper role for plays and movies to play with reference to the Study. However, these plays and movies should be based on the facts and should accurately represent the roles of all the participants. I had the privilege of seeing such a play while in Los Angeles, California, in October 1997. *The Trees Don't Bleed In Tuskegee* was written by Duane Chandler while he was a student at Syracuse University. In researching the play, he came to Tuskegee and interviewed several of the participants and other persons in the community, including me as their attorney. I had the privilege of reviewing the manuscript before it was produced by Spencer Scott and presented by the Unity Players Ensemble of Los Angeles.

In my opinion, the play is factual, the drama is good, and it is an accurate portrayal of the participants. It also sends the correct message. It places the responsibility of the Study squarely upon the United States government. There is no effort to shift blame from the government to Nurse Rivers, to any African American doctors, or to anyone else. It simply "lets the chips fall where they may." Plays like this one, which accurately depicts what occurred in the Tuskegee Syphilis Study, need to be known and need to be made into movies.

Media Tells the Story

Fortunately, the inaccurate movie *Miss Evers' Boys* has been just one small part of the worldwide media attention that has helped spread the word about the Study. From the day the Study was made known in 1972, there has been substantial press coverage. The extent of the coverage undoubtedly influenced the speed and the extent of the government's response once the spotlight was turned on.

The initial coverage was short lived, and an occasional story appeared in the media until about a year later when I filed the suit and requested $1.8 billion for the participants and their heirs. Again, there was some press coverage, but it subsided. When the case was settled in 1975, there was limited coverage.

The Study and the lawsuit have been the subject matter of various television productions, theater productions, and the previously mentioned book, *Bad Blood,* by Jim Jones. The television productions included a documentary produced by NOVA for PBS Television in 1993, a European production by Diverse Productions of London, England, in 1992, and a featured segment on ABC-TV's "Prime Time Live" in 1992. Mr. Herman Shaw was on the Donahue Show in New York in 1995.

9

The Presidential Apology

When I became counsel for the Tuskegee Study participants in 1972, my immediate priorities were to (1) stop the Study; (2) obtain treatment for the living men; and (3) obtain compensation for them and their heirs. As it turned out, the first of these took care of itself. Public pressure forced the end of the Study within a few months of its exposure while we were still researching the facts of the lawsuit. The various experts appointed by the Department of Health, Education, and Welfare also moved quickly to provide medical attention, and we subsequently made sure in the legal settlement that this care would be comprehensive and life-long. Compensation was also provided for in the settlement.

However, as counsel to the men, my colleagues and I had concerns that went beyond the lawsuit. We wanted to make sure that what happened to these men would not be forgotten and that some lasting good would come from the Experiment. In part, these concerns were addressed by the widespread publicity, by the various hearings, and by the legislative and regulatory actions that resulted. After the disappointment of *Miss Evers' Boys,* we realized that it was important that the nation fully understood what had happened, realized the extent of the injustice that had been committed, and made symbolic amends for it.

The matter of making amends was realized in the Presidential apology that occurred at the White House on May 16, 1997. "No power on Earth can give you back the lives lost, the pain suffered, the years of internal torment and anguish. What was done cannot be undone. But we can end the silence. We can stop turning our heads away. We can look you in the eye and finally say on behalf of the American people, what the United States government did was shameful, and I am sorry," said President Clinton.

The significance of this apology for the surviving participants and their families cannot be overestimated. Ironically, the events leading up to the apology contained some of the same lack of openness and the same undemocratic thinking that conceived the Study in 1932. For as the maneuvering toward the apology began, the Study participants were once again left in the dark and completely ignored.

Background of the Apology

I received a phone call from a news reporter in February 1997 asking me when President Clinton was going to make an apology to the participants in the Tuskegee Syphilis Experiment. The reporter assumed that since I represented the men, I would have some knowledge of the proposed apology. I did not. In fact, I was really shocked to hear that such a move was in the making without the involvement of the participants.

More calls came from other reporters, convincing me that this was more than a rumor. When the original reporter made a follow-up call, I commented that other reporters had been calling. Then it was her turn to be surprised. She said she had merely been "floating a trial balloon" with me about a tidbit she had heard from a source. I later learned from an article in *Jet* Magazine that around this time the Congressional Black Caucus had asked the President to make an apology, which perhaps was behind the inquiries.

However, about the same time, Mr. Charlie Pollard's niece called and said someone from the Centers for Disease Control in Atlanta was coming over to see him. The CDC was the administrator of the Health Care and Death Benefit Program for the Study participants and certain of the heirs. I have an abiding interest in this program as I insisted that the health care program be made a part of the settlement agreement in *Pollard v. United States* to ensure that the benefits would continue regardless of changes in the White House or Congress. During the years immediately after the settlement, I knew the young ladies who worked on a day-to-day basis with the participants quite well. They kept me advised, and I kept them advised on the needs of the participants. However, as the CDC medical care became routine and as the number of surviving participants dwindled over the years, so did my contact with the Centers for Disease Control.

But, we learned that the CDC was also planning to visit other Study participants. Various members of my staff made arrangements to be present at these interviews, and afterwards we concluded that the CDC was checking on the participants' health. This was done periodically. However, this could also determine whether the participants were in condition to travel to Washington, D.C. and learn the participants' current opinions of the health care program. During the interviews, no mention was made of an apology.

Within the next few weeks, two important events happened:

First, I discovered that some eighteen months earlier, a Tuskegee Experiment Legacy Committee met on the campus of Tuskegee University, with one of its purposes to seek a Presidential apology. The committee was established without any input from or involvement by the Study participants. They were completely ignored. This was troublesome to them and to me because this is typical of what whites have done to African Americans over the years. In too many cases, whites believed that they knew what was best for blacks, and blacks did not have to be consulted. Now, African Americans are following the patterns set by whites; now we don't consult each other.

Second, *Miss Evers' Boys* was shown on television, and several of the surviving participants held a conference at my law office to view a tape of the movie and to discuss a response. They asked me to write a letter [see appendix] to President Clinton advising him that the participants joined with others in requesting an apology. The letter should also ask that a permanent memorial be built in Tuskegee to recognize the role of the Study in the movement for human and civil rights. Finally, if the President elected to make such an apology, they wanted to be included in the planning and to take an active part in any apology ceremony.

In addition, they asked me to arrange a press conference at one of the sites where they had been recruited for the study in 1932 so that they could tell the nation what they wanted as a result of their participation; they also wanted the country to know that they were joining with others in requesting an apology; and they also wanted to tell the nation that *Miss Evers' Boys* was inaccurate and did not properly portray them or Nurse Rivers.

In essence, the surviving participants, all men now in their nineties, decided they wanted to take control of any further public discussion of their lives. They asked me to help them, which I was only too happy to do. The first person I discussed this with, of course, was my wife, Bernice. Together, we began to make plans to implement their desires. We talked about it, prayed over it, and concluded that we would go ahead with the press conference the men had requested.

Participants' Press Conference

The press conference was held April 8, 1997, in Notasulga at the Shiloh Missionary Baptist Church, the church Mr. Charlie Pollard attends and where he was recruited for the Study sixty-five years earlier.

We felt that given the opportunity and enough background information to whet their interest, the media would want to see the men, talk with them, see some of their family members, and learn why the men wanted a presidential apology. Press releases were prepared and sent, and on the day before the press conference, the news media was already pouring into Tuskegee and Macon County. On April 8, the day of the press conference, State Highway 81 from Tuskegee to Notasulga was very busy.

Rev. Hall, pastor of the Shiloh church, welcomed everyone to the church and led the singing of "Old Time Religion," prayed, and introduced me. I thanked all who made the press conference possible* and explained that we held it at Shiloh Missionary Baptist Church because it is the site where

---

*These included the officials of the church; Shirley Johnson, a very active worker in the community; Deborah Gray; Joanne Bibb, my administrative assistant; and other members of our staff who were present, including Trudy Powell, Fred D. Gray Jr., Bridget Gray, Ernestine S. Sapp, Walter E. McGowan, Stanley F. Gray, and Allan Nathanson. Elected

Charlie Pollard was recruited as a participant in the Tuskegee Syphilis Experiment, several of the participants are buried in the nearby cemetery, and the church had been the community focal point for obtaining the right to vote. I recognized the 623 participants of the Experiment, and introduced the living participants who were present: Charlie Pollard, Herman Shaw, Carter Howard, Fred Simmons, and Ernest Hendon. We also recognized the 615 men who had died, along with my wife, Bernice, who had passed recently. We had a moment of silent prayer on behalf of all of them.

I gave a brief history of the Study and made several major points: the production of *Miss Evers' Boys* was wrong; the participants wanted to join in the request for an apology; and the participants wanted to have constructed in Tuskegee a permanent, physical, structure that would not only recognize the contributions they made, but also the contributions that other persons have made in the human and civil rights field. Then I introduced the participants, and Mr. Shaw made remarks.

The press then asked questions. 1. What difference would it make if the President issued an apology to you and the rest of the men? Mr. Shaw answered, "It would make a great contribution, because we figured we have been left out and used as guinea pigs. And, so, we would be very appreciative, if he made the apology." 2. You mentioned the State of Alabama's role; would a presidential apology also eradicate the need of some similar to the apology? Are you asking Governor [Fob] James to do the same? I answered, "We hadn't asked Governor James to do the same. I think you raised a very interesting question, because the State of Alabama did participate from its inception. After penicillin became available, there was a meeting in Montgomery with the State Health Officials and they decided to continue the program and not to administer the penicillin to us. It would be appropriate if Governor James apologized."

---

officials who were present and were recognized included Tuskegee Mayor Ronald Williams; Macon County Commission Chairman Jesse Upshaw; Sheriff David Warren; Macon County Board of Education members Conna Bradford and Stanley F. Gray; Auburn School Board member Clina White. Sergeant Willie R. Whitehead, vice president of Macon County Greyhound Park, was also recognized.

There were also questions from the audience, and several family members of the participants in the Experiment. Family members of the deceased participants also voiced their views.

When the press conference ended, many pictures were made. The men were moved to the fellowship hall for refreshments and continued to be available to the media for pictures and interviews. In my opinion, the media did an excellent job of covering the press conference. After the press conference, some media persons saw and filmed the school where the early meetings were held. Some made pictures at the cemetery and others did their stories from that site.

Immediately the Tuskegee Syphilis Experiment was a top story of the major newspapers across the nation and around the world. It was also a lead story on all networks that evening and the next morning. As a result of the press conference, in less than six hours, the White House announced that President Clinton would make an apology.

The hard work of the past two months had paid off. The press conference was a success.

Preparations for the Apology

The next day, I received a telephone call from White House liaison Ben Johnson indicating that the President would make an apology to the participants. No details were available, but I was assured that the White House would be in contact and the participants would be involved.

One concern of the Administration was whether the living participants and some family members of deceased participants could travel to Washington if the ceremony was held at the White House. Of course, if the ceremony was held in Tuskegee, more local people could be involved. I wanted the apology to occur in Tuskegee for the following reasons: (1) the wrong to be addressed had occurred in the Tuskegee Macon County community, and it would substantially help the healing process, if the President could come to the same area where the wrong occurred, and look us all in the eye and make the apology; (2) consideration should be given to the living participants whose ages ranged from eighty-seven to more than one hundred years.

Notwithstanding our request, it quickly became apparent that the apology would take place in Washington. We were assigned the task of gathering the security clearance information of the living participants and their escorts. Each participant would be able to invite one person as his escort. The Centers for Disease Control handled arrangements for family members of deceased participants. The Centers for Disease Control would also be responsible for the transportation, hotel accommodations, and other incidental expenses for all persons attending.

The next few weeks were intense. Arrangements were made for travel and for a satellite broadcast of the ceremony to be held simultaneously at Tuskegee University so local persons could participate. We fielded many media requests for interviews.

Two last-minute interviews I was especially happy to arrange. Nationally syndicated radio talk show host Tom Joyner is a Tuskegee native and a graduate of Tuskegee University. I did not mind getting up at 5:55 a.m. on May 15, 1997, to be on his show, to tell his national audience about the history of the Study and that in a few hours four of the eight living participants would be leaving for a meeting with the President. I was also happy for Karen Gray Houston, my niece who is a news reporter with a Washington, D.C., television station to interview me and Mr. Herman Shaw about why this apology was important. I explained that even though the government had settled the lawsuit and paid compensation, it had never acknowledged responsibility. Even though it was a long time coming, the apology meant that the federal government which planned, executed, and financed this inhumane program for over forty years, had finally decided to admit liability. I was happy that the government acknowledged, notwithstanding how powerful it is, it also makes mistakes. This is the way it should be. It strengthens our faith and confidence in our government.

As I prepared to board the bus that would take us to the Atlanta airport, I felt an emptiness that I could not quite overcome. My wife, Bernice, who had been by my side for more than forty years, who motivated me, and who helped me with this case and even with the strategy behind the press conference which moved the President to respond, would not be able to accompany me to Washington, because the Lord had seen fit to call her. She died unexpectedly on March 18, 1997.

The Trip to Washington

This would be the first time in the nation's capital for most of those going, and the historic significance of the events that were to occur had everyone in a state of high excitement. We were accompanied by staff members of the Centers for Disease Control—including a doctor in case anyone got ill. On the bus to the Atlanta airport were four participants: Mr. Charlie Pollard, Mr. Herman Shaw, Mr. Carter Howard, and Mr. Fred Simmons. Joining us at the Atlanta airport was Mr. Frederick Moss who is a living participant and at that time lived in a nursing home in Glencoe, Alabama (he now lives in a nursing home in Tuskegee). Also on the bus were Gwendolyn Cox, Bernice Tolbert, Eva Parker, Joanne Bibb, Fred Simmons, James Michael Simmons, Fred D. Gray, Fred D. Gray, Jr., Fannie Mitchell, Dora Banks, Lucille Smith, Ola Tolbert, and David Allen.

After we were settled on the bus there were several announcements. Rosa Putman of the Centers for Disease Control's Health Care Benefit Program, coordinated the trip with the participants, the widows, and heirs. She gave us an overview of the trip and introduced several other CDC staffers who were along to make sure that the participants, the widows, children, and grandchildren would be comfortable, and that their needs would be met. They wanted to make this not only a historical trip, but also an enjoyable one.

Joining us in Atlanta for the flight to Washington were Dr. William C. Jenkins, Manager of the CDC's Participants Health Benefit Program, and several other nurses, family members of participants, CDC staffers, and news media.

We had an uneventful trip, arriving in Washington late in the afternoon. We checked into our hotel rooms and those who could relax for a while did so, while others of us responded to the continuing multitude of media interview requests.

When I arrived in my room there were twenty-five telephone messages from various media people. Of course, we did not want to offend any of the news people, because we needed them, not only to continue to get our message out about the participants in the Experiment and the apology, but for the work that lay ahead in connection with the development of the Tuskegee Human and Civil Rights Multicultural Center. I went through that list of twenty-five calls and returned each one of them. Among the calls was one from Congressman John Conyers of Michigan. I have known Congressman Conyers for many years. When Mrs. Rosa Parks left Montgomery in the 1950s, she went to Detroit, Michigan, and was given a job in Conyers's office. I had close ties with him. He wanted me to meet with members of the Congressional Black Caucus prior to the White House ceremony on Friday so that we all would be unified in terms of what we wanted in addition to the apology. I told him of the plans for the Tuskegee Human and Civil Rights Multicultural Center. He wanted me to talk with Congressman Louis Stokes of Ohio and Congresswoman Maxine Waters of California. I told him where I was, and he said he would arrange a meeting with them at my hotel. I have known Louis Stokes of Cleveland for many years. I was a good friend of his brother, Carl Stokes, former mayor of Cleveland, where I went to law school.

That evening we had a very nice time at a reception held in the participants' honor by the National Bar Association. President Lawrence Bozé, Executive Director John Crump, and many other African American lawyers from the Washington area were present. I am a former president of this national lawyers' group, which dates back to the time when black lawyers were not allowed membership in the American Bar Association.

Immediately after the reception, we convened a business meeting with the participants and heirs. I brought them up to date on the formation of the Tuskegee Human and Civil Rights Multicultural Center. Then there was a meeting with Dr. David Satcher, director of the Centers for Disease Control, who has subsequently become the Surgeon General of the United States. Dr. Satcher is an Alabamian. He answered questions about the CDC and outlined the schedule we would follow the next two days.

Later that evening I met with Congressman Louis Stokes of Ohio and Congresswoman Maxine Waters of California. I gave them a package which contained a copy of my statement to be released after the apology ceremony, the statement of participant Herman Shaw, and a copy of the Articles of Incorporation for the Tuskegee Human and Civil Rights Multicultural Center. Stokes and Waters indicated that they would support what we were trying to do and asked me to keep them informed.

The Day of the Apology

The next morning, we went by bus to the White House. The five living participants and their escorts, the family members representing the three living participants who couldn't make the trip, and my son Fred Jr. and I were escorted into the Blue Room for a private meeting with President Clinton and Vice President Gore. The others in our group were escorted directly to the East Room to await the actual ceremony.

As we entered the front door of the White House, a military band was playing chamber music. A military escort carried us into the Blue Room. Finally the President and the Vice President came and greeted us. They went to each individual, shook hands, exchanged greetings, and posed for photographs.

When the President came to me, I reminded him about the book I had given him in 1996. He said, "Oh yes, I remember *Bus Ride To Justice*. You gave it to me when I was in Birmingham." I laughingly told him that I "just happened" to have a photo of the time I presented it to him and would appreciate his autographing it. He wrote: "To Fred Gray—With gratitude for your lifetime of labor for freedom and equality. Bill Clinton." He expressed his appreciation for the work I had done for the participants over the years, and was delighted that I was able to accompany them to the ceremony.

After we met the President, we were escorted into the East Room and seated at the front of the assembled rows. There was a brief, expectant wait, and I am confident that everyone there was reflecting on the historic nature of the events that were unfolding. I know I was. I was also thinking that I was present because God had given me the opportunity to serve the participants as their attorney.

The role of civil rights lawyers is an interesting one. I knew from long experience that once a civil rights legal victory is accomplished, everybody somehow assumes that it just happened. Often there is no real understanding for the role of the lawyers and staff members who work very, very hard on legal matters involving civil and human rights. Hours upon hours of time went into the lawsuit over the Tuskegee Syphilis Experiment. In recent months, it took tremendous amounts of time and effort to make sure that the media were appropriately courted, nourished, and encouraged to come and cover the press conference in Notasulga, which set the stage for the Presidential apology. We knew that if we could get the media to come to Notasulga, the participants—Herman Shaw, Charlie Pollard, Carter Howard, and Fred Simmons—would sell themselves. They are truly men, men with pride, men with a deep feeling of commitment. I knew that they would be able, in their own humble ways, to present themselves in such a fashion that we would all be proud. And they did.

Apology Ceremony

Everyone was seated in the East Room. The band played "Hail to the Chief" and the President, Vice President, and Dr. Satcher entered. The President greeted Mr. Shaw, whom I had selected to speak for the participants and was seated on the podium. This was a very impressive scene. On the side and in the back were what seemed to be hundreds of media representatives. On the right side, there were dignitaries and further over in another section included delegates from the Congressional Black Caucus, White House personnel, other Congresspersons, and African American presidents of various organizations invited by the President.

Vice President Gore opened the ceremony by welcoming the guests* to the White House and giving the order of the program for this very important ceremony. He welcomed the five living participants present, and indicated that they would be individually recognized later.

---

*The five living participants; the heirs of deceased participants; Congressman John Glenn; Congresswoman Maxine Waters of California, the Chair of the Congressional Black Caucus, Congressman Louis Stokes from Ohio, who works with the Congressional Black Caucus on health issues; the Secretary of Labor, Alexis Herman, from Mobile, Alabama; Rodney Slater, Secretary of Transportation; and the heads of many African American organizations

Vice President Gore commented on the tragedy of the Experiment, saying, "Medical professionals willingly and intentionally let human beings suffer from a treatable, and then later a curable illness . . . It was a disgraceful episode for American scientists. We feel the repercussions still, tremors of distrust that have not yet disappeared. To this day, the Tuskegee Study makes some Americans think twice about donating blood, taking their children for vaccinations or signing an organ donor card. But out of this sad incident, we can learn, we can find healing, and we can vow that such hideous episodes will never occur again."

He introduced Dr. Satcher, who said, "Today is a historic event. As our President acknowledges the tragedy of the U. S. Public Health Services' Syphilis Study in Tuskegee and apologize on behalf of the government for decisions made many years ago that still haunt us, we open a new chapter in public health. . . . The race for scientific discovery is important, but must never overshadow our commitment to human dignity. We must hold ourselves to the highest ethical standards, never stop monitoring our progress, and always be open to public scrutiny, and willing to admit our mistakes."

Dr. Satcher introduced Mr. Herman Shaw.

Mr. Shaw received a standing ovation, which he richly deserved. As I sat and listened to Dr. Satcher introduce Mr. Shaw, I reflected on the first time he came into my office. Twenty-five years earlier, none of us would have believed that Mr. Shaw would not only have won his case and a place in United States' history, but he would have the rare opportunity of personally meeting and shaking hands with the President, having photographs taken with him, being escorted into the East Room of the White House, greeted and embraced by the President, and now, in one of the greatest moments of his life, he had the opportunity of making remarks and introducing the President. That is the kind of involvement that the participants deserved.

---

that were invited to attend the ceremony. He also acknowledged the presence of the heads of many organizations in the health care field, particularly those who fought to eradicate AIDS, including acknowledging the presence of Dr. Benjamin F. Payton, President of Tuskegee University, and Dr. Henry Foster, former obstetrician and a resident of Tuskegee, who was nominated for Surgeon General.

Mr. Shaw said he was speaking on behalf not only of those who were in the audience but also of those who could not attend, some of whom had died during the Study. He thanked President Clinton for inviting the group to the White House. He then went on to say:

> It has been over sixty-five years since we entered the program. We are delighted today to close this very tragic and painful chapter in our lives. We were treated unfairly—to some extent like guinea pigs. We were not pigs. We were not dancing boys as we were projected in the movie, *Miss Evers' Boys*. We were all hard working men, and not boys, and citizens of the United States. The wounds that were inflicted upon us cannot be undone. I am saddened today to think of those who did not survive and whose families will forever live with the knowledge that their death and suffering was preventable.
>
> Mr. President, we want to also thank our lawyer, Attorney Fred Gray, [standing ovation] who has represented us during these twenty-five years, and who has helped to make this day possible.
>
> This ceremony is important because the damage done by the Tuskegee Syphilis Study is much deeper than the wounds any of us may have suffered. It speaks to our faith in government and the ability of medical science to serve as a force for good.
>
> As I said at the press conference at Shiloh Missionary Baptist Church in Notasulga, on April 8, in addition to an apology, we want to construct in Tuskegee a permanent memorial. A place where our children and grandchildren will be able to see the contributions that we, and others, made to this country. I am glad that I helped form the Tuskegee Human and Civil Rights Multicultural Center which will be for the purpose of creating such a lasting memorial.
>
> In my opinion, it is never too late to work to restore faith and trust. And so, a quarter of a century after the Study ended, President Clinton's decision to gather us here; to allow us to put this horrible nightmare behind us as a nation, is a most welcomed decision.
>
> In order for America to reach its fullest potential we must be one America—black, red and white together, trusting each other, caring

for each other, and never allowing this kind of tragedy which happened to us in the Tuskegee Study to ever occur again.

Mr. President, words cannot express my gratitude to you for bringing us here today—for doing your best to right this tragic wrong, and resolving that America should never again allow such an event to occur again.

Ladies and gentlemen, I give you the President of the United States.

There was another standing ovation for Mr. Shaw. To see Mr. Shaw so ably address the issues that he needed to touch in making remarks about the Study was exhilarating. This certainly was the highlight of his life, and one of the highlights of mine. When Mr. Shaw acknowledged me as the participants' attorney and for helping to make this day possible, I received a standing ovation from those present in the East Room of the White House. It was a very humbling experience for me and very moving, as it was a few minutes later when President Clinton recognized me, saying, ". . . a great friend of freedom, Fred Gray, thank you for fighting this long battle for all these long years." I wish Bernice could have been there. When I accepted this case some twenty-five years ago, I never thought about an apology. I never thought about a ceremony at the White House. I never thought that one of the participants would ever have the privilege of personally visiting the White House, shaking the President's hands, making pictures with him, and expressing his views on the tragedy of his involvement, and the involvement of his colleagues in the Tuskegee Syphilis Experiment. I just wanted to help the men who had been mistreated and betrayed.

I sat on the front row on the right side facing the podium. I had a good view of Mr. Shaw presenting the President. I observed the thundering applause with everyone standing. As I watched the President come to the podium, there was a great moment of anticipation. This is the moment the participants hoped for, prayed for, and waited on for sixty-five years. It was about to happen. Year after year and time after time, the participants were mistreated, ignored, taken advantage of, but now they were the stars and were about to hear the President of the greatest nation in the world express to them, their families, the Macon County community, and to the world the official position of the United States government.

President Clinton then gave a tremendous speech. It was sincere; it was factual; it was filled with emotion; it was from the heart; and at points, there were tears in his eyes. He did not bite his tongue in expressing the wrongs committed by the government.

This was a powerful, emotional moment for many in the room, and it certainly was for me. As I listened to the President, I remembered that first day when Mr. Pollard came into my office wanting me to help him. He was saddened and angry by what his federal government had done to him. Over the next quarter century I worked on his behalf and that of the other 622 participants. The long battle began with the filing of the lawsuit in the Middle District of Alabama arguing that these men had been betrayed and their constitutional rights had been violated. Now, twenty-five years later, we were at a White House ceremony and the President was saying what we had said then. The more I listened to the President speak, the more over-come with emotion I became.

The President said the "survivors of the syphilis study at Tuskegee are a living link to a time not so very long ago that many Americans would prefer not to remember, but we dare not forget." The President further stressed the importance of remembering the past even though shameful, but it is necessary in order that we may amend and repair our nation; and without remembering it, we cannot make amends and we cannot go forward.

He then proceeded to make the apology.

Speaking directly to the participants, and families who were involved, he not only apologized for their involvement, but for the length of time it took the apology to come. He extended it "to Macon County, to the City of Tuskegee, to the doctors who had been wrongfully associated with the event that took place, Tuskegee University, and to the larger African American community." As I stated earlier in this book, Tuskegee Institute (now Tuskegee University), Nurse Rivers, and the entire community were taken advantage of. The President recognized this and he apologized to them.

After the President made this apology, he then did what I believe to be the initial commitment for bringing people together. He stated, that what happened in the Tuskegee Syphilis Experiment "can never be allowed to happen again." Because "it is against everything our country stands for and what we must stand against is what it was."

The President acknowledged that this study has done a great deal to divide our people, and that we cannot ignore a whole segment of our nation, because the nation must be built on trust, not just on one segment of the community but all of it. So, the presidential apology is simply the first step. Then he proceeded to announce five other steps that would be done.

First, the government would help to build that lasting memorial at Tuskegee Mr. Herman Shaw was talking about in his remarks. The President further announced that the Department of Health and Human Services will award a planning grant to Tuskegee University for establishing a center for bioethics and research and health care.

Secondly, the President said that the government is committed to increase its community involvement so that it may begin restoring lost trust, and the study at Tuskegee will assist in that regard. He further stated that he was directing the Secretary of Health and Human Services, Donna Shalala, to issue a report in 180 days about how the government can best involve communities, especially minority communities, in research and health care.

Third, the government committed itself to strengthening research training in bioethics.

Fourth, the government pledged to increase and broaden our understanding of ethical issues and clinical research. The government committed itself to providing post-graduate fellowships to teach bioethics especially among African Americans and other minorities. Those fellowships will begin in September of 1998. Finally, by executive order he was extending the charter of the National Bioethics Advisory Commission to October of 1999. That Commission is charged with the responsibility of finding ways to further strengthen the protections for subjects in human research.

He concluded his speech by saying:

> We face a challenge in our time. Science and technology are rapidly changing our lives with the promise of making us much healthier,

much more productive and more prosperous. But with these changes we must work harder to see that as we advance we don't leave behind our conscience. No ground is gained and, indeed, much is lost if we lose our moral bearings in the name of progress.

This was a tremendous speech. It was and is the beginning of the healing process. The President began by saying, "I am sorry." He concluded by saying "only you have the power to forgive."

The Simulcast

The apology ceremony was telecast live on CNN. A special satellite feed was set up and sent to Tuskegee University, where it was shown live in the Kellogg Conference Center, thus including in the day's events many local people who were not able to make the trip to Washington. Foremost among these were Study participants Mr. Ernest Hendon and Mr. Sam Doner, and family members. Mr. Doner's health was so poor that he had to be brought by ambulance and wheeled into the Kellogg Center in a hospital bed. He has since died. That Mr. Doner would come to the simulcast in such a delicate health condition is a witness to the personal meaning of the apology to the men who were involved.

Post-ceremony Press Conference

In my opinion, these men truly have forgiven. As counsel for the participants, I made a statement after the ceremony [see appendix] thanking the living participants and their families for coming to Washington, and for their participation in the program. I extended my personal appreciation to the President for the apology.

In addition to my address to the press, Dr. Payton, the President of Tuskegee University, and many other persons made comments. The news of the presidential apology was a prominent story across the nation in the evening news. It was also the front page headlines in all majornews papers on Saturday, May 17, 1997, with a picture of the President embracing Mr. Herman Shaw during the ceremony.

As I looked back at the ceremony and as I indicated in my letter to the

President on behalf of the participants on May 21, 1997, after thanking him for the apology I said, "Your consoling words and forthright candor with reference to the Study and the sincere way you spoke and apologized will remain forever in our hearts. You are truly a President who cares for all of the citizens of the nation. On their behalf, we humbly and respectfully accept the apology, and forgive the government for its misconduct." So the President has apologized, and he said on behalf of the country he was sorry. He said to the participants "only you have the power to forgive," and they have forgiven. Now we move on towards the establishing of that permanent memorial in Tuskegee.

Once the ceremony ended, the participants and all of the other persons went to the State Dining Room of the White House for a reception. Later they boarded buses and returned to the hotel. They could enjoy the balance of the day at their leisure. I spent the evening answering media questions and looking forward to where we go from here.

The next morning we packed early and made arrangements for the return trip to Tuskegee. First, the bus ride from the hotel to the airport. During that ride I had one final opportunity to speak not only to those who had come with us from Tuskegee, the five participants, but there were some others who came from other places from across the country who were also on the bus going to the airport. I conducted a business meeting as we went to the airport. In the meeting they ratified and confirmed the fact they wanted me to write a letter to the President accepting the apology. I told them that I would also write them and keep them posted on what we were doing in connection with the Tuskegee Human and Civil Rights Multicultural Center. They again ratified and confirmed the fact that what they were interested in is that a permanent memorial be established in Tuskegee and their support of the Tuskegee Human and Civil Rights Multicultural Center.

Going back to Tuskegee, we had an opportunity to think about the last forty-eight hours. They were full; they were rewarding; they were enriching. It was a step back into history and a leap into the future. No one knows where it is going to end, but it is well on its way towards being what it should be. The plane trip from Washington to Atlanta was quiet. Everyone was reflecting on what had happened. We exchanged conversations with all of the people on the bus and the plane and from Washington to Tuskegee.

We decided since the next day was Mr. Shaw's birthday to have a party. CDC staffers made arrangements to have a birthday cake ready for him in Tuskegee upon our arrival. Upon our arrival, we went to our office in Tuskegee, and had a birthday party for Mr. Shaw. We had a big cake, sang happy birthday, and expressed our appreciation for the manner in which he delivered the remarks on behalf of the participants. It was a grand day.

10

The Legacy

What a difference twenty-four years make. When the lawsuit on behalf of the participants was filed in 1973, the United States of America was willing to admit only that the participants in the Study were African American, it began in 1932, and it was conducted by the government. The speeches by the President, the Vice President, and the Surgeon General at the apology ceremony in 1997 revealed a 180-degree turn.

Vice President Gore said the experiment was one of the "most shameful chapters in the history of American medicine," that the methods used by the government were "irredeemably cruel," that "medical professionals willfully and intentionally let human beings suffer from a treatable and then later a curable illness." To this day, he said, "the Tuskegee Study makes some Americans think twice about donating blood, taking their children for vaccination, or signing an organ donor card."

Dr. Satcher continued where Vice President Gore left off. He stated that the Study was "wrong for many reasons: the Study participants were never informed about the purpose of the Study, never asked to give their informed consent to participate in the Study, and were intentionally misled about receiving treatment."

The President put the icing on the cake by candidly laying the blame for the Study directly on the federal government. He stated, "Men who were poor and African American, without resources and with few alternatives, believed they had found hope when they were offered free medical care by the United States Public Health Service. They were betrayed." He further stated, "For forty years, hundreds of men were betrayed, along with their wives and children, along with a community in Macon County, Alabama, the City of Tuskegee, the fine university there, and the larger African American community. The United States government did something that was wrong—deeply, profoundly, morally wrong. It was an outrage to our commitment to integrity and equality for all our citizens."

After the ceremony, Mr. Shaw said, "Listening to the President speak from his heart about the Experiment, I was happy and it felt like a burden was lifted. I felt proud to be an American."

When Mr. Shaw stood after the President finished, the President embraced him. To witness the President of the United States, with tears in his eyes, embracing Mr. Shaw was indeed a great and momentous occasion. The apology ceremony gave powerful witness to how important this case was to the persons involved in it, not only for the financial remuneration they received, the medical care, and burial expenses, but for safeguards that have been written so that other persons would not become victims of similar experiments. The significance of this case was that the United States of America, while initially not admitting to wrongdoing, was willing to compensate the aggrieved parties. This case also demonstrated that the judicial process is a viable means of rectifying wrongs perpetrated against citizens of this country regardless of their race and economic status. The case reaffirmed the principle that prior informed consent should be obtained from individuals before they are allowed to participate in human experimentations. As a result of this, and the enactment of laws after some of the participants testified before a Senate Committee, the government has re-evaluated the use of human beings in experiments and has set minimum standards in order to conduct human experimentations.

These events are a part of the legacy of the Tuskegee Syphilis Study.

Two tangible legacies to the Study are being created in Tuskegee. One is the Tuskegee Human and Civil Rights Multicultural Center which was mentioned by Mr. Herman Shaw in his remarks at the ceremony and further detailed in my remarks at the press conference following. The other is the Bio Ethics Center at Tuskegee University, which was referred to by President Clinton in his remarks at the apology ceremony.

The Tuskegee Human and Civil Rights Multicultural Center

Mr. Shaw stated in his remarks that the participants wanted a prominent memorial constructed in Tuskegee acknowledging the contributions which they and others have made toward human and civil rights. Toward that end he has assisted in forming the Tuskegee Human and Civil Rights Multicultural Center. President Clinton later stated he would help build that center.

My wife, Bernice, and I realized a long time ago that Tuskegee and Macon County were uniquely suited for a large-scale educational memorial which would help American citizens understand and appreciate the richness of their diverse cultures. Throughout the centuries, the three major ethnic groups of Native Americans, European Americans, and African Americans have made history in Macon County and Tuskegee.

Macon County typifies, in many ways, the history of American diversity. It was populated first by Native Americans. Then Europeans came, some bringing African American slaves. Eventually the Native Americans were driven from their homes. Afterwards thousands more whites came and even more African American slaves. Then a war was fought over slavery, and African Americans gained their physical if not their economic and civic freedom. Then another war was fought, this one with the weapons of law and non-violent protest, so that African Americans could have political freedom. Many of the events of that war are described in *Bus Ride to Justice*.

Tuskegee was also the site of the pioneering educational work of Booker T. Washington, George Washington Carver, C. G. Gomillion, and many other great leaders. Tuskegee was also the site where the Tuskegee Airmen proved during World War II the bravery and contributions of African Americans in the field of military aviation.

The Tuskegee Syphilis Study is a part of this history, an unfortunate part, to be sure, but one that could be turned to good through an educational effort. As I said, Bernice and I felt this years ago, but it was simply a question of how to do it.

After viewing *Miss Evers' Boys* and talking with the surviving Study participants about their desire for the Tuskegee memorial that would tell the truth of the Study, we made plans for a non-profit, tax exempt organization to educate and perpetuate the contributions made to Tuskegee, Macon County, and the nation by Americans of African decent, Native Americans, and Americans of European decent.

The Tuskegee Human and Civil Rights Multicultural Center was incorporated in May 1997 as an Alabama tax-exempt nonprofit corporation. Mr. Herman Shaw represents the Study participants on the Board of Directors and, despite his advanced age, has been a vital and active member of the planning process.

The Alabama Exchange Bank in Tuskegee recently donated to the Center a building in downtown Tuskegee. Robert Davis is the president and CEO of the bank, and he stated that the donation was to help create the permanent memorial Mr. Shaw talked about at the White House.

Bernice did not live to see this, but I am now working with the participants to build the Tuskegee Human and Civil Rights Multicultural Center. The Center will bring together people of all races and acknowledge the contributions of their cultures.

In addition, such a Center in downtown Tuskegee will be an economic boost for Tuskegee. The hundreds of thousands who visit the campus of the Tuskegee Institute National Historic Site could come downtown to the Tuskegee Human and Civil Rights Multicultural Center, and be able to see the contributions that these people have made in the field of human and civil rights. This could motivate them to stay in the City of Tuskegee for hours, probably spend the night, and spend some money in Tuskegee.

This is a very ambitious project and will cost millions of dollars to develop fully. When the residents of the city of Montgomery started the Montgomery Bus Boycott it was a very ambitious project, but it launched the Civil Rights Movement. History, particularly civil rights history, records many such accomplishments.

Toward its goal of healing divisive racial wounds, the Tuskegee Human and Civil Rights Multicultural Center is calling for the financial support of the federal government, the state, foundations, corporations, organizations, and individuals in the construction of the Center as a permanent legacy of significant achievements in the areas of human and civil rights. Particularly, we are calling upon the federal government for technical assistance in planning such a permanent legacy of the Tuskegee Syphilis Study.

The Bioethics Center

President Clinton announced that "the Department of Health and Human Services will award a planning grant so the school (Tuskegee University) can pursue establishing a center for bioethics in research and health care. The Center will support efforts to address the legacy of the Study and to strengthen bioethics. In February 1998, the University announced it had received $4.1 million in federal grants that will go towards a Bioethics Center.

Tuskegee University President Benjamin Payton pushed for the Center following President Clinton's apology to survivors of the Tuskegee Syphilis Study. According to newspaper accounts, Dr. Payton said he hoped "the Bioethics Center at the University will be operating and fully staffed within three years." He also stated, "one mission would be to address 'the legacy of mistrust of medical research institutions that lingers from the Syphilis Study.'" On April 2-3, 1998, at Tuskegee University, I attended a workshop entitled "The Principles of Bioethics" which was designed to give an overview of the subject to those who will be involved in establishing the proposed Tuskegee University Center For Bioethics in Research and Health Care. The workshop gave participants a better understanding of the basic principles of bioethics, as well as an opportunity to apply those principles in a workshop setting. The sessions included (1) an ethical situation, (2) a case study involving the participants' discipline, (3) a statement regarding the participants research interest, (4) concerns about specific roles related to establishing the Center. Guest lecturers were Dr. Annette Dual, who presented "Ms. Mildred"; Dr. Marian Secundy, who discussed the history of bioethics; and Dr. September Williams, who discussed clinical decision making. There were small group discussions and a debriefing.

11

Beyond Tuskegee

During the course of President Clinton's apology, he directed Secretary of Health and Human Services Donna Shalala "to issue a report in 180 days about how we can best involve communities, especially minority communities, in research and health care. Every American group must be involved in medical research in ways that are positive. We have put the curse behind us; now we must bring the benefits to all Americans."

Pursuant to the President's directive, a meeting was held in Atlanta, Georgia, with a broad cross-section of individuals to assist the Secretary in making her report on how "we can best involve communities, especially minority communities, in research and health care." However, none of the participants in the Study were invited to this important meeting which was to report on ways to increase community involvement so that "lost trust" could be restored. Even after the apology, it seems that the government is still not actively involving the participants in activities which are designed to restore trust.

Many organizations are doing many things in the names of the participants in the Tuskegee Syphilis Study. Many proposals have been written and some funded in the name of or as a direct result of the persons in the Tuskegee Syphilis Study. Yet, in virtually none of these instances have the participants themselves been contacted or given an opportunity to be involved. As we move beyond Tuskegee, if there is to be true healing and if trust is to be restored, that trust and restoration must include the participants and their views in every stage.

Race and Scientific Experimentation

One of the greatest tragedies would be for the nation to discover that notwithstanding the apology wrongful scientific experiments are still occurring in the African American community. On February 19, 1998, the Lorraine Hansberry-Robert Nemiroff Archival Educational and Cultural Fund sponsored a Race and Science Forum entitled *Beyond the Tuskegee Experiment: Race and Scientific Experimentation in the Black Community*. This program was held at the New York Public Library's Schomburg Center for Research. I was invited by Jewel Gresham Nemiroff, president of the Hansberry-Nemiroff Fund.

The program was moderated by Utrice Leid, host of *Talk Back*, WBAI-FM, New York. The facilitator was Dr. Benjamin Roy, III, chief of psychoneuroimmunology research at Albany Medical College. The forum was summarized for the Hansberry-Nemiroff Fund by Matthew Lyons, who reported:

> • Dr. Roy discussed the long history of commercially driven medical research, from the centuries-old use of human cadavers to the close ties between the African slave trade and the early spice trade (which included commerce in scarce medicinal herbs. He noted that, historically, medical researchers in the U.S. and elsewhere have often abused or disregarded ethical constraints on their work.
>
> • Science reporter Neenyah Ostrom spoke about AIDS research and racism. She stated that some researchers have portrayed AIDS (like syphilis in an earlier period) as having different symptoms and transmission rates in whites and blacks. She described a study in which the AIDS drug AZT—which has been found to have significant health risks, including an increase in birth defects—was given to pregnant women, of which three-quarters were African American or Latino, a fact she attributed to racism. She said women who participated in that study were not told of the health risks. She noted that researchers are

planning to conduct AIDS vaccine experiments in Africa and Asia that would be considered unethical in the U.S.

• Community health activist Loretta Jones described a situation in Los Angeles in 1989 in which 1,500 infants, mostly African American or Latino, were given an experimental measles vaccine yet their parents were not told that the vaccine was experimental, nor was the clinical trial halted when concerns were raised that the vaccine was increasing the mortality rate among infants at sites in Africa and Haiti. She also described a second example of a clinical trial of possible AIDS vaccines in Los Angeles, focusing on African Americans as a population at "high risk" of contracting HIV/AIDS.

• Dr. Peter Breggin, director, International Center for the Study of Psychiatry and Psychology, discussed abusive psychiatric research and treatment, with particular emphasis on racism. He related claims by some psychiatrists and neurosurgeons in the 1960s that African Americans participated in riots because of "brain disease" which supposedly could be surgically corrected. Such ideas were revived in the early 1990s with the Federal Violence Initiative, which involved efforts to find biological or genetic indicators of violence among inner city youth.

• Dr. Pauline Lane, senior lecturer, University of East London, spoke about genetic prospecting in the Third World—the large-scale search for commercially exploitable human tissue samples, particularly from isolated indigenous communities, with little or no ethical oversight.

Each of the panelists at this forum stated that scientific experiments are still being conducted in the African American community, not only in this country, but around the world. Some experiments that would be illegal if conducted in this country are being conducted with U.S. funds on human beings in other countries.

The point I am making by all of this is that we must be very diligent to be sure that what happened in the Tuskegee will never happen again.

12

Epilogue

I wrote this book primarily to tell the real story of the Tuskegee Syphilis Study from my perspective as a veteran civil rights lawyer who was the attorney for the participants. The real story belongs to Mr. Pollard, Mr. Shaw, the other 621 participants, and family members who I was privileged to represent.

In addition to receiving compensation, health care, funeral expenses, and the apology, these men want a memorial erected in Tuskegee so that what they endured will be a reminder to the nation of the dangers of unethical medical research. To that end, the participants, represented especially by Mr. Shaw, have created the Tuskegee Human and Civil Rights Multicultural Center. The Center will not only memorialize the Study and the participants, but will be a powerful educational resource about the roles of the various ethnic groups that have contributed to Macon County, the region, and the nation.

I am committed to seeing that these objectives are implemented. As we travel beyond the Tuskegee Syphilis Study, the Center can be the vehicle by which we remember and celebrate our shared history—the bitter along with the sweet. As we move forward and make progress in the health care field, let us remember the lessons learned from the Study. We must prevent experiments similar to the Tuskegee Syphilis Study from happening.

Another question that is frequently asked about the Study is a personal one: Since I have represented these men for twenty-five years, how has it affected my life? Well, in 1972, I was in the prime of life, forty-two years of age, married to a lovely young lady who had worked by my side since prior to our marriage on June 17, 1956. We had four lovely children: Deborah, Vanessa, Fred Jr., and Stanley, who at that time the lawsuit began were ages fifteen, fourteen, eleven, and eight. I was a member of the Alabama Legislature, a civil rights lawyer, Minister of the Newtown Church of Christ in Montgomery, and had a full schedule. I recognized that this case was one of the most important cases in my career, and so did my wife. We committed ourselves to do everything that could be done to be sure that justice would be accomplished for these men and their heirs. In addition, I wanted to be sure that those who were living were compensated, be provided with free health care for the rest of their lives, and have their funeral expenses paid at their death. I also wanted to be sure that the heirs of the deceased participants were compensated. We started from scratch. Everything looked dim, and as I discussed earlier, we had to overcome tremendous difficulties.

In a broader sense, this case gave me a tremendous amount of national exposure, for I had the opportunity to travel to all parts of the country and several countries abroad to talk not only about the Tuskegee Syphilis Study but about discrimination and the civil rights movement in this country.

In addition, this case afforded me the largest fee of my career up to that point. At that time, I had been practicing as a civil rights lawyer for eighteen years. I had received a great deal of gratification in tearing down the walls of segregation, but had earned very little money. So, economically, this case assisted me and my family and strengthened our law firm. Incidentally, my two sons are now partners in my firm, and one of my daughters and a daughter-in-law also work in the firm. I have been blessed by having my family close to me in my personal, church, and vocational life.

I am always mindful that but for Bernice Gray, we may never have developed the case and moved it to its fullest potential. She played a tremendous role in telling the story of the Tuskegee Syphilis Study because she worked and lived with it up until her sudden death. Through the Center and in other ways, she will continue to make her contributions. They are immeasurable.

Appendix

Table of Contents

Appendix A

Documents Relating to the Study,
1932–1972

Introduction to the Tuskegee Study

R. A. Vonderlehr, M. D.

During the 20-year period from 1891 to 1910, Professor Caesar Boeck, Chief of the Syphilis Clinic at the University Hospital in Oslo, Norway, hospitalized 2200 patients with primary or secondary syphilis until their lesions healed without treatment. This was prior to the advent of the arsphenamines and he felt that the patient's defense mechanism could combat disease more effectively than the antisyphilitic treatment of his day. In 1929 Bruusgaard, former assistant and successor to Boeck, startled the medical world with his report on the fate of these patients 15 to 40 years after their infections. His data indicated that of every 100 patients with untreated syphilis 10 would develop neurosyphilis, 13 cardiovascular syphilis, and 12 benign late syphilis, but that 64 would pass through life apparently unharmed. Furthermore, in 28 of the 64 "spontaneous cure" would occur. As with all retrospective studies, many flaws were found in these data. The principal objection to their validity was the fact that Bruusgaard was able to obtain information on only 22 percent of the original patients.

In this present age of antibiotics in which numerous drugs will effect a cure for syphilis, the importance of these findings may appear vague. It must be remembered, however, that at the time of Bruusgaard's report there was no standard treatment for syphilis. Although the arsphenamines were considered specific therapy, they were, by and large, administered in a haphazard manner as often as patients presented themselves and for as long as patients could be persuaded, or could afford, to remain under treatment. Furthermore, there was evidence to indicate that such erratic treatment probably did more harm than good.

Stimulated by a survey conducted in 1928–1930 by the Health Section of the League of Nations, the cooperative Clinical Group composed of leading syphilologists, standardized a procedure for the treatment of early syphilis in the United States. In general, this consisted of weekly injections of an arsenical and bismuth administered in alternating courses for a period of 70 weeks. For comparative purposes in evaluating the efficacy of this treatment, a group of untreated syphilitics was desirable. Although the Bruusgaard study had just been published, these data did not seem applicable to the situation in the United States. A large percentage of our infected population was Negro and with even our limited knowledge of that time we were aware that in this group syphilis more frequently attacks the cardiovascular than the central nervous system. We were also aware that although cardiovascular conditions could easily be detected their etiology could rarely be determined prior to autopsy.

Between 1929 and 1931 the Public Health Service in cooperation with local health departments and the Julius Rosenwald Fund had surveyed six rural areas in the South. The highest prevalence of syphilis (398 per 1,000) was found in Macon County, Alabama. Of the 1400 cases admitted to treatment during the survey, only 33 had ever had previous antisyphilitic therapy and the average for these 33 was less than 5 arsenical injections.

This group was far from being an ideal control group, for just as the Bruusgaard study was based on only 22 percent of the original patients, this group represented merely a segment (the survivor) of an unknown number of individuals who had been infected with syphilis. In spite of this drawback, it was felt that this group afforded a unique opportunity to study the late effects of untreated syphilis on morbidity and mortality. It was also anticipated that through intensive clinical and laboratory study culminating in autopsy this group would make an invaluable contribution toward establishing criteria for the diagnosis of cardiovascular syphilis.

Approximately 400 syphilitic male volunteers were solicited for study. Only those were included who had at least positive serologic tests for syphilis and a history of a primary lesion. To prevent further occurrence of congenital syphilis, women were treated and excluded from the study, as were young males with recently acquired infections. All participants were over 25 years of age, the majority over 40. The group included, therefore, only those who had already passed through the critical period of syphilis without therapy and who would be at slight risk to themselves or to the community if treatment continued to be withheld.

A control group of apparently 200 nonsyphilitic males of similar ages, serologically and clinically negative for syphilis, who gave no history of early lesions, were selected for study from the same population group. The Tuskegee Study was thus composed of approximately 600 participants and our long-range goal was to follow each until autopsy.

To accomplish this a full-time Public Health Service nurse was assigned to the Macon County Health Department. Her primary duty, under the guidance of the local health officer, was to keep track of each of the 600 men in the study. Once a year a medical officer of the Public Health Service was to make a progress investigation, consisting of a cursory physical examination and serologic tests for syphilis of each participant. Complete physical examinations were to be performed at approximately 5-year intervals.

When a participant in the study died, consent of the family was sought for autopsy. It was soon learned that most of the deceased were not attended at death by a licensed physician and that the cause of death was given by the local registrar. A small fee was paid to a local registrar for notifying the county health officer of the death of a study group man before a burial permit was issued. A portion of the cost of the funeral has also been paid to the family of the deceased after autopsy has been completed.

The gross necropsies have been done by the pathologist at the Tuskegee Veterans Administration Hospital and the microscopic studies performed by pathologists at the National Institutes of Health. Funds for the autopsies and procedures incidental thereto have been provided by the Milbank Memorial Fund. The professional staffs of the John A. Andrew Memorial Hospital at Tuskegee Institute and of the local Veterans Administration Hospital have also rendered valuable assistance as consultants.

References

1. Gjestland, Trygve. "The Oslo Study of Untreated Syphilis," *Acta Dermatovener* 35, Supplement 34 (1955).

2. Bruusgaard, E. "The Fate of Nonspecifically Treated Syphilitic Patients," *Arch. f. Dermat. u. Syph.* 157 (1929): 309.

3. Stokes, John H., et al. "Standard Treatment Procedure in Early Syphilis," *Ven. Dis. Inform.* 15 (1934): 4.

4. Clark, Taliaferro. *The Control of Syphilis in Southern Rural Area.* Chicago: Julius Rosenwald Fund Publication, 1932.

5. Vonderlehr, R. A., et al. "Untreated Syphilis in the Male Negro," *Ven. Dis. Inform.* 17 (1936): 260.

Appendix B

Documents and Statements Relating to the April 8, 1997, Press Conference

March 31, 1997, Press Release

GOVERNMENT APOLOGY FORTHCOMING
IN TUSKEGEE SYPHILIS STUDY?

Remaining participants in the Tuskegee Syphilis Study, the 40-year experiment financed by the United States government and conducted by the United States Public Health Service to observe the effects of untreated syphilis in African Americans, will seek an audience with the President and an apology from the government at a news conference on April 8, 1997, at 10 o'clock A.M., at Shiloh Baptist Church, Notasulga, Alabama, one of the collection sites for the participants in the Study.

Accompanied by Attorney Fred D. Gray, legal counsel for the participants in the Study, the men will also express their views and concerns in relation to injustices depicted in the recently aired HBO film, *Miss Evers' Boys.* "This movie is in no way representative of the actual events which I endured for 40 years," said Charlie Pollard, lead plaintiff in the lawsuit against the United States government and other entities for wrongful acts conducted during the Study.

"To allow men to suffer and die in the name of science is insidious and vile," said Gray. "HBO's depiction of the men is equally disheartening. It is an intolerable distortion of history. Ironically, *Miss Evers' Boys* was initially aired during Black History Month on February 22, President Lincoln's birthday. This movie has been shown repeatedly through the powerful means of television, stereotyping Black images even further before a mass audience. Not only is it a cruel affront to the survivors of the Tuskegee Syphilis Study and the descendants of all the men, but equally an affront to the entire African American community," Gray further stated.

"There is a reason that African Americans and other minorities do not participate in large numbers in test programs for cures of diseases and illnesses." Gray commented further, "aside from their frequently simply not being considered, many remember all too well the Tuskegee Syphilis Study and the inhuman treatment of the 600-plus African American men."

DIRECTIONS TO SHILOH BAPTIST CHURCH

Shiloh Baptist Church is located on Alabama Highway 81, approximately 8 miles North of downtown Tuskegee, Alabama. Exit off Interstate 85-North at the Tuskegee-Notasulga ramp (Exit 38), proceed North on Highway 81 approximately 5 miles to Shiloh Baptist Church on the right.

Statement of Fred D. Gray

Press Conference
April 8, 1997
Shiloh Missionary Baptist Church
Fred D. Gray has represented the participants in the Tuskegee Syphilis Study
from July, 1972, to date. This statement is being released during a press conference
held at Shiloh Missionary Baptist Church, in Notasulga, Macon County, Alabama,
on April 8, 1997. In addition to Attorney Gray and members of his law firm, the
following participants of the Study are also present: Charlie Pollard, Herman Shaw,
Carter Howard, Fred Simmons, and Ernest Hendon.

THE FIRST TRAUMATIC EXPERIENCE

Sixty-five years ago, beginning in 1932, the United States Government, through
its public health service, committed one of the greatest frauds, injustices, and mis-
representations against 623 African-Americans who were citizens of Macon County,
Alabama. The men were misled into participating in a study of untreated syphilis
sponsored, financed, and supported by the federal government for over 40 years.
The government induced these men to participate in a program in which the government represented that the participants were being treated for whatever their
ailments were, even though they were not told the ailment. They never gave their
consent to be involved in the Study, nor did they realize that they were a part of a
Study until the story broke in July of 1972. There were no rules or regulations
governing the Study. Available at this press conference is a copy of Chapter 17 of
Bus Ride To Justice by Fred D. Gray, published by Black Belt Press. This chapter sets
forth in detail the facts and circumstances surrounding the Study. An accurate
account of the Study can also be found in *Bad Blood* by James H. Jones.

In July 1972, Fred D. Gray began to represent these participants and on July
24, 1973, filed a lawsuit which was amended on August 1, 1974.

In 1974, the lawsuit was settled, and the Government agreed to pay approximately seven million dollars to the living participants and the heirs of the deceased
participants. Subsequent to the disbursement of these funds, interest on the proceeds has also been disbursed to the participants and heirs. In total, more than
6,000 persons have shared in the settlement. As a part of the settlement agreement,
the government was ordered to continue its program of providing health care for
the living participants and some widows of participants for the rest of their lives,
and to provide free burial service for the participants at their death. The government also terminated the Study.

As a result of the publicity, Congress passed laws which prohibit similar occurrences to what occurred in the Tuskegee Syphilis Study. Safeguards are now in

place to ensure that what happened to these men will never happen to any other human being.

The government's persuasion of these men to participate in the Study was the first traumatic experience that occurred in 1932. Other traumatic occurrences have happened since then with regard to these men.

THE SECOND TRAUMATIC EXPERIENCE

On February 22, 1997, during Black History Month and on President Lincoln's birthday, Home Box Office telecast its premiere of a movie called *Miss Evers' Boys*. Allegedly, *Miss Evers' Boys* was based on the facts involving the participants in the Tuskegee Syphilis Study. The film does not accurately portray the facts of what occurred to the participants in the Tuskegee Syphilis Study. Thus, the premiere showing of *Miss Evers' Boys* and its repeated showings were another great tragedy which occurred in the lives of these men. On Monday, February 24th, four of the participants reviewed *Miss Evers' Boys* and the following are their comments and the comments of their counsel, Fred D. Gray, on some of the inaccuracies and how they feel about *Miss Evers' Boys:*

1. They were startled, amazed, and very unhappy about the way in which they were projected in the movie. They feel unanimously that the film does not accurately portray the events and circumstances of the Tuskegee Syphilis Study as they participated in it, and as they observed Miss Eunice Rivers, the nurse involved in the Study.

2. The movie opened by stating that these men were solicited to participate in a program for treatment of syphilis, and that they were treated over a period of time until such time as the money for treatment became unavailable. The movie further stated that treatment was discontinued for the lack of funds. However, according to the movie, money became available to study untreated syphilis in the men. The fact is, the participants in the Tuskegee Syphilis Study were never treated for syphilis from the beginning of the Study until the end.

3. The film showed a Dr. Brady, an African-American physician who was projected as the supervisor of the Study, and Miss Rivers' immediate supervisor. There was no such African-American who generally supervised Miss Rivers nor the Study. All of the supervisors were white. The persons who conceived and presented the matter to the health service for financing were all white. The doctors who actually came to Macon County and examined these individuals were all whites, and not African-Americans. The white Macon County health officer, Dr. Murry D. Smith, accompanied Miss Rivers when they were recruiting participants for the Study.

4. The entire emphasis of the film tends to shift the blame from the federal government to an African-American doctor and an African-American nurse. This

Study was conceived, financed, executed, and administered by the federal government. The African-American professionals who participated in it were victims as were the 623 African-American participants.

5. The film conspicuously omits the role that the State of Alabama, through its Board of Health, played in the Study. The Alabama Health Department cooperated with the federal government in continuing not to treat the participants after penicillin became available, notwithstanding the fact that Alabama laws required such treatment.

6. In the film, there were four men who were projected as "Miss Evers' Boys." They, basically, were projected as musicians and dancers, and they represented the other 619 men who participated in the Study. That is not true. The men who participated in the Study, for the most part, were hard working, reputable persons in their communities. Each of my clients, after reviewing the film, stated, Miss Rivers was always professional and courteous to them. She did not accompany them to night clubs. They did not dance, play music, and entertain people at night clubs with Miss Rivers. The entire depiction of them as dancers and "shuffling sams" is a great misrepresentation, and does not accurately represent them, nor the other persons who were participants in this study.

7. From this general representation of these four men, not only will viewers of the movie think that they were representative of the other 619 men who were in the Study, but viewers would also believe that these men were typical of African-Americans who lived in Macon County at that time and even now. It is a tremendous insult and a gross misrepresentation of projecting African-American men as being typical of those projected as the four "Miss Evers' Boys."

8. There is nothing in the historical account and nothing that these men remember observing about Miss Rivers which would indicate that she had a love affair with one or more of the participants as it was set forth in the film. Miss Rivers did not give penicillin to one participant and withhold it from all the others.

DON'T SUBJECT THE PARTICIPANTS OF THE TUSKEGEE SYPHILIS STUDY TO A THIRD TRAUMATIC EXPERIENCE

Some 65 years after the Study began and over 25 years with knowledge of the Study, local and national community support of these participants has finally come by way of requesting that the federal government make an apology to these individuals for the harm, embarrassment, and injuries that it has caused them and their heirs. I am informed that several persons and organizations have requested that the government make an apology to these men. We understand that the Honorable Donna Shalala, Secretary of Health and Human Services, has discussed this matter with the President. The participants and their counsel join in the request for such an apology. To date, no official contact has been made from the federal government to the participants nor their counsel concerning an apology. The participants have some views concerning an apology.

In additional to an apology, the participants believe that they should be appropriately recognized for their contributions to the nation.

In a letter to President Clinton dated March 26, 1997, as counsel for the participants I stated:

There are eight living participants, the youngest of whom is 87 years old. In view of the fact that these men and their heirs have suffered substantially, the remaining participants and I would consider it an honor to meet with you to discuss an appropriate manner to resolve the issue. On behalf of these men, we are ready, willing, and able to share their views with you or your representatives at your convenience.

In 1932, these men were taken advantage of by being used as human guinea pigs. Their lives were placed in jeopardy as part of a Study on the effects of untreated syphilis without their knowledge and consent. Sixty-five years later, they have been entirely misrepresented in the manner they are projected in *Miss Evers' Boys*. They are now requesting that an appropriate apology be made, and they be recognized for the contributions they made to the nation.

On Monday, April 7, 1997, counsel for the participants received a telephone call from The White House. He was informed that his letter was received and was under consideration. Counsel believes that the President will act favorably upon our request.

Statement of Mr. Herman Shaw, April 8, 1997

Mr. Shaw:

And for those of you who have come to make up this body, we are happy you are here. However, we are not so happy with what we're about to say, but thank you for coming.

First I will say something about the Study and then I'll get on to my subject. My subject is *Miss Evers' Boys*. However, I don't see or I haven't been able to find out in my searching how *Miss Evers' Boys* came to be a part of this program that we were in. We suffered through it. Everybody received the same treatment.

Now, coming to *Miss Evers' Boys* and Miss Rivers—it has aggravated me. It makes me think how wrong it was. Having seen the movie, things like that never existed. It's just something that was added to the movie. Now, Nurse Rivers never carried anybody to a dance hall. She never carried anybody to these drunk places and things of that kind. And those boys hadn't been in the program that we were in. I don't know how they got in there, but it was wrong. It's a formality. It's just wrong. Now, we—we suffered through a number of years and we want to be recognized. I think that we as people should be recognized. We are all born under the same administration. We are all born free men—freedom of choice. We want to be recognized by having a permanent monument in Tuskegee. We would like to be recognized in Tuskegee. We would like to have—you go around ride up and down Highway 80 and see historical signs. We want to make history. We would like to become recognized in Tuskegee so that our children, grandchildren, and great grandchildren will see what we went through. I'm thinking we would like to go to the President and let the President recognized us—he and his staff and the U.S. government.

Again, I would like to say that *Miss Evers' Boys* has been a disgrace to this program. We never had anything like that during the time we were in the study. Another thing, we were discriminated against. All the student doctors that came out from the North every four years—and they were all white. I would like to say we were treated inhuman at times. Nobody knows what we went through with except those of us who are living participants right today. Now, I tell you, I cannot get *Miss Evers' Boys* off my mind because it's wrong. I can't see how they got in there. But, anyway, allow me to say if you will, *Miss Evers' Boys* and what they said about Miss Rivers was absolutely wrong. It was not in (the program). So, we had a program. They gave us all the same medicine. The same capsule. The same tablets. Now, again, may I say, penicillin, it wasn't even issued. Those of you who have seen the picture heard penicillin mentioned, we didn't have that kind of treatment. May I say, again, those of you who saw Nurse Rivers going out getting all those people in dance halls and all that kind of stuff, it did not happen. I'm a living witness. I lived through it and I thank the Lord for it.

Now, I would like to say we are most appreciative of our attorney, Fred Gray, for he stayed with us. I hope that he'll continue on with us. Again, I say we are glad to have Charlie Pollard and others here. We'd like to say again we appreciate you all coming and appreciate the opportunity.

Question and Answer Period, April 8, 1997

Gray: I hope when I get to be 94, I can talk like that. Are there any questions? You all have come from all over the country and we're just appreciative to you and we wouldn't dare have you leave without giving you an opportunity to ask some questions. Yes?

Question: What difference would it make if the President issued an apology to you and the rest of the men?

Shaw: It would make a great contribution to the study because we figure we've been left out and used as guinea pigs. And so we would be very appreciative if someone said I am sorry.

Question: Mr. Shaw, I just wanted you to sort of describe why it is that if you were able to talk to the President in person today, what would you tell him? Why would you want that apology?

Shaw: I really want an apology because of recognition and the simple reason we went through the same thing that other people went through with. Allow me, if you will, let me give you a little historical background. The colored man has served in every war that has ever occurred in the United States. Look how long it took just even—just last year—that he became recognized to what—to get a monument up in the cemetery. And that's why we want to be recognized.

Gray: I think the concern is probably multifaceted. There's no question but this happened. It only happened in a Black community and it only happened to Blacks or African Americans. We think there should be a recognition that what was done was wrong. You know when you file a lawsuit and people settle, they'll give you some money, but they say, "we deny any liability," but here's some money and let's get the lawsuit over. But, one of the problems with our country today is we commit wrongs and when the government commits a wrong, we never acknowledge the fact that it's wrong. One of the major problems wrong in this country right now is still racism. But people don't want to recognize it as racism. They will tell you that everything is fine because they can go and buy a hamburger now, even though I can't get a job to get the money to buy the hamburger. So I think that recognition on the part of the government that it's wrong is very important. I think it should be a concern, not just for these few men who are here, but a concern for all of us that our government would participate in something like this and every year or so we find something else happened. This isn't the—I tried during discovery of this case to get the court to have the government disclose all of the studies it was involved in. And, of course, the judge didn't permit that. We think it is of real importance and concern. I think the fact that all these people are here, and the fact that the media is here as you are, you don't usually come from all over the country to a little place like Notasulga for nothing. So I think your presence here is indicative of some concern.

Question: Mr. Shaw, could you address that issue? There are a number of people who are here who have said they are here out of concern. I'm wondering how you are interpreting that. The presence of so many people here—that there are eight of you who are able to talk about your experience. How do you interpret that concern here?

Shaw: I think they are concerned because no doubt some have seen the movie, *Miss Evers' Boys,* and it needs to be corrected.

Question: Mr. Shaw, why do you think this particular area, you and your colleagues were chosen? Why this particular group of 623 men?

Shaw: Really to begin with, I didn't have the thought at that time back in '32, but I think it's a shame and disgrace to think about Macon County, one of the most outstanding counties in the State of Alabama, and throughout the world as well. There were times in 1932, or say 50 years ago, if a student graduated from here he went on and got a job. Let one graduate now; how long will it take him to get a job? I don't think people should discriminate against Macon County and its participants.

Question: I'd like Mr. Shaw to tell us—do you remember how you were recruited? Can you talk about that?

Shaw: I'd be glad to. In 1932, President Hoover was President of the United States. And those of you read about it, you read about our political system. I lived through it by the help of God. Those of us who lived in the rural area, we could not get a doctor; couldn't get medicine or anything of that kind. Dr. Murry Smith, the Macon County Health doctor and Nurse Rivers saw me at Simmons Chapel and said that poor people could get medicine and things of that kind.

Gray: What happened in Simmons Chapel is another church that's about eight or ten miles away from here. But, throughout this county Miss Rivers and Public Health officer Murry Smith indicated, and there were some little leaflets that had been circulated earlier, saying there was a new health care program and they were soliciting persons to be involved in that health care program. It's my understanding that actually they examined and interviewed several thousand individuals. We don't know the criteria these doctors used in selecting the 623 that they selected.

Question: Did you know that something was the matter with you?

Shaw: No. no. They did not tell us, we had no knowledge. They never did tell us we had syphilis. They never did tell us what they were treating us for.

Question: Mr. Gray, Mr. Shaw, we know how some people feel about an apology. Would an apology bring you peace and closure?

Shaw: It would not climax the thoughts and peace of that kind but we would consider the case closed with an apology. We would like to be recognized; we would like to have recognition.

Question:

I would like to direct a question to Mr. Shaw. I am curious. In the early Fall when Mrs. Rivers used to bring the guys out to the V.A. Hospital—what did they do to you all? I'm curious. All the years I was never able to find out. I did question Mrs. Rivers. What did the V.A. do to you all when you came out once or twice a month. Do you remember?

Shaw: I don't recall once or twice a month. I do recall every four years. However, I would say they gave us [electra]cardiograms and things of that kind which would necessitate about an hour and a half or two hours. At noon time they gave us our dinner.

Appendix C

Statements and Documents
Relating to the Apology

Vice President Al Gore, May 16, 1997

Please be seated, ladies and gentlemen. On behalf of the President and the First Lady, it is an honor to welcome all of you to the White House for this very important occasion. I wish to begin, and on behalf of the President acknowledge the distinguished guests, beginning with the five survivors who will be named individually by the President and the families of other survivors who are represented here with us today and one of them will be, Mr. Shaw, will be introduced by Dr. Satcher in a moment, and he will present the President. I wish to acknowledge the many members of congress who are present, Senator John Glenn, the Chair of the Congressional Black Caucus, Congresswoman Maxine Waters, the Congressman representing the district from which most of these individuals traveled, Congressman Earl Hilliard, and Congressman Louis Stokes, who figured prominently in the effort to address this injustice, and some thirty-five other members of the Congressional Black Caucus, all of whom worked together, tirelessly, to make certain that the people of the United States of America were made fully aware of the need for the step the President is taking today. Members of the cabinet, Transportation Secretary Rodney Slater and Labor Secretary Alexis Herman, other distinguished guests—I can't mention all by name, but there are the heads of a great many prominent African American organizations in the United States of America, the heads of many organizations formed to battle against the threat of AIDS, organizations that have also been prominent in the efforts of individuals such as Dr. Henry Foster, Dr. Benjamin Payton, President of Tuskegee University, and dozens of other extremely distinguished prominent guests, too many to acknowledge individually.

Six decades ago, indifference and injustice combined to begin to write one of the most shameful chapters in the history of American medicine, of course, the infamous project called the Tuskegee Study of Untreated Syphilis in the Negro Male. In 1932, America's Public Health Service set out to study syphilis, but it pursued this worthy goal in a manner that was irredeemably cruel. Several hundred African-American men, men the Public Health Service recruited at churches and clinics and farms were used in the study. Most of these men had syphilis, none of them knew their bodies harbored this disease. And then the Public Health Service followed the men's lives, watched how the disease developed, all the while withholding medicine, withholding treatment of any kind for these innocent American citizens.

Medical professionals willingly and intentionally let human beings suffer from a treatable, and then later a curable illness. These researchers knew that mercury and arsenic compounds could treat the disease, but the Tuskegee men did not receive the medicine. Later the researchers knew that penicillin could cure the disease, but, again, the Tuskegee men did not get the medicine. They didn't get treated until the forty-year study was discovered and stopped amid public outcry in 1972. It was a disgraceful episode for American scientists. We feel the repercussions still, tremors of distrust that have not yet disappeared. To this day, the Tuskegee Study makes some Americans think twice about donating blood, taking their children for vaccinations or signing an organ donor card. But out of this sad incident, we can learn, we can find healing, and we can vow that such hideous episodes will never occur again.

The relentless pursuit of scientific truths is a noble endeavor, but not so noble that it exempts us from our deeper obligations to be moral and just to revere the sanctity of the lives of our fellow men and women. The ultimate purpose of science is to improve human lives. Science and technology can be powerful forces for good and usually are. They have cured diseases, built economies, helped to narrow the distance of time and space. In the 21st century as the march of new discovery picks up even more speed, we must be vigilant about making certain science and technology always remain positive forces in American life. So today the nation, under President Clinton's leadership, at his initiative, finally does the right and the honorable thing.

It is now my pleasure to introduce and bring to the microphone one of the people who has led this effort that has brought us here today. The distinguished Director of the Centers for Disease Control and Prevention, Dr. David Satcher.

Dr. David Satcher, May 16, 1997

Thank you Mr. Vice President, Mr. President. I am honored to be here today with you and all of our distinguished guests. As I begin my remarks, I'd like to make a few acknowledgements. First of all, I would like to recognize the acting Surgeon General, Dr. Audry Manley, who is participating in the ceremony by satellite from Tuskegee, Alabama, along with several of the Study participants and their families who are unable to attend the ceremony in Washington, D.C. So our satellite down link is working.

I want to especially thank the Secretary of Health and Human Services, Donna Shalala, who is giving a commencement address and could not be with us today, but her leadership has allowed us to raise the standards of human research. And, finally, I would like to thank President Clinton for his courage, his commitment, and vision in bringing us together so that we can make a new beginning.

We see it as an opportunity to start again sensitized by the lessons we have learned from past mistakes and continuing to enhance our mission to protect the public's health. Today is an historic event. As our President acknowledges the tragedy of the U. S. Public Health Services' Syphilis Study in Tuskegee and apologizes on behalf of the government for decisions made many years ago that still haunt us.

We open a new chapter in public health. The U.S. Public Health study of untreated syphilis in the Negro male was wrong for many reasons. The Study participants were never informed about the purpose of the Study, never asked to give their informed consent to participate in the Study, and were intentionally misled about receiving treatment. By publicly admitting our mistakes, and acknowledging the role of the Public Health Service in the Study, we have an opportunity for a new beginning.

The future will also bring new ethical challenges. We must be prepared to meet them and to meet them together. As a nation, we must ensure that anyone who conducts human research receives comprehensive bioethics training and understanding and incorporates the principles of bioethics in their work. In those local communities where the research is conducted, are treated as full partners as we strive to uphold the highest ethical principles. But if history has taught us anything, it is that these principles are meaningless if we don't apply them fairly and equally across all lines of race, religion, and gender. The race for scientific discovery is important, but must never overshadow our commitment to human dignity. We must hold ourselves to the highest ethical standards, never stop monitoring our progress, and always be open to public scrutiny, and willing to admit our mistakes.

As Secretary Shalala said this morning in her commencement address at the

University of Wisconsin School of Medicine: "We must insure that our ethics are always as sophisticated as our science." So, to the survivors and their spouses and family members who are watching from Tuskegee, Alabama, and those who are here with us in Washington, D.C., we want to thank you for your willingness to participant in today's ceremony. You are allowing us to come together, and you are giving us this opportunity to chart a new beginning. It would have been easy for you to take a cynical attitude towards this event. Instead, by being here today, you express hope for the future, the kind of hope which we need to transmit to our children.

Now I would like to introduce the next speaker, a very special person, Mr. Herman Shaw, one of our honored guests and a participant in the Tuskegee Syphilis Study. Mr. Shaw was an original participant in the Study, and he participated for forty years. He was married to Fannie Mae Greathouse for sixty-two years. They have two children, both college graduates, he has six grandchildren, and one great grandchild. He told me last night that for the last fifty-two years, he has been driving his tractor, and he already has his garden in place for this year. Welcome Mr. Herman Shaw.

Mr. Herman Shaw, May 16, 1997

Thank you, thank you, thank you very much, thank you very, very, much.

On behalf of all the survivors who are here today, and those who could not attend, and on behalf of the heirs of my fellow participants who have died, I wish to thank President Clinton for inviting us to the White House. It has been over 65 years since we entered the program. We are delighted today to close this very tragic and painful chapter in our lives.

We were treated unfairly and to some extent like guinea pigs. We were not pigs. We were not dancing boys as we were projected in the movie, *Miss Evers Boys*. We were all hard working men, not boys, and citizens of the United States. The wounds that were inflicted upon us cannot be undone.

I am saddened today to think of those who did not survive and whose families will forever live with the knowledge that their death and suffering was preventable.

Mr. President, we want to also thank our lawyer, Attorney Fred Gray, who has represented us during these 25 years, and who has helped to make this day possible.

This ceremony is important because the damage done by the Tuskegee Study is much deeper than the wounds any of us may have suffered. It speaks to our faith in government and the ability of medical science to serve as a force for good.

As I said at the press conference at Shiloh Missionary Baptist Church in Notasulga, on April 8, in addition to an apology, we want to construct in Tuskegee a permanent memorial. A place where our children and grandchildren will be able to see the contributions that we, and others, made to this country. I am glad that I have helped form the Tuskegee Human Rights Multicultural Center which will be for the purpose of creating such a lasting memorial.

In my opinion, it is never too late to work to restore faith and trust. And so, a quarter of a century after the Study ended, President Clinton's decision to gather us here, to allow us to finally put this horrible nightmare behind us as a nation, is a most welcomed decision.

In order for America to reach its fullest potential we must truly be one America—black, red, and white together; trusting each other, caring for each other, and never allowing the kind of tragedy which happened to us in the Tuskegee Study to ever occur again.

Mr. President, words cannot express my gratitude to you for bringing us here today—for doing your best to right this tragic wrong, and resolving that America should never again allow such an event to occur.

Ladies and gentlemen, I give you the President of the United States.

President Bill Clinton, May 16, 1997

Ladies and gentlemen, on Sunday, Mr. Shaw will celebrate his 95th birthday. I would like to recognize the other survivors who are here today and their families: Mr. Charlie Pollard, Mr. Carter Howard, Mr. Fred Simmons. Mr. Simmons just took his first airplane ride, and he reckons he's about 110 years old, so I think it's time for him to take a chance or two. I'm glad he did. And Mr. Frederick Moss, thank you, sir.

I would also like to ask three family representatives who are here—Sam Donar is represented by his daughter, Gwendolyn Cox. Thank you Gwendolyn. Ernest Hendon, who is watching in Tuskegee, is represented by his brother, North Hendon. Thank you, sir, for being here. George Key is represented by his grandson, Christopher Monroe. Thank you, Chris.

I also acknowledge the families, community leaders, teachers, and students watching today by satellite from Tuskegee. The White House is the people's house; and we are glad to have all of you here today. I thank Dr. David Satcher for his role in this. I thank Congresswoman Waters and Congressman Hilliard, Congressman Stokes, the entire Congressional Black Caucus. Dr. Satcher, members of the Cabinet who are here, Secretary Herman, Secretary Slater. A great friend of freedom, Fred Gray, thank you for fighting this long battle all these long years.

The eight men who are survivors of the syphilis study at Tuskegee are a living link to a time not so very long ago that many Americans would prefer not to remember, but we dare not forget. It was a time when our nation failed to live up to its ideals. when our nation broke the trust with our people that is the very foundation of our democracy. It is not only in remembering that shameful past that we an make amends and repair our nation, but it is in remembering that past that we can build a better present and a better future. And without remembering it, we cannot make amends and we cannot go forward.

So today America does remember the hundreds of men used in research without their knowledge and consent. We remember them and their family members. Men who were poor and African American, without resources and with few alternatives, they believed they had found hope when they were offered free medical care by the United States Public Health Service. They were betrayed.

Medical people are supposed to help when we need care, but even once a cure was discovered, they were denied help, and they were lied to by their government. Our government is supposed to protect the rights of its citizens; their rights were trampled upon. Forty years, hundreds of men betrayed, along with their wives and children, along with a community in Macon County, Alabama, the City of Tuskegee, the fine university there, and the larger African American community.

The United States government did something that was wrong—deeply, profoundly, morally wrong. It was an outrage to our commitment to integrity and equality for all our citizens.

To the survivors, to the wives and family members, the children and the grandchildren, I say what you know: No power on Earth can give you back the lives lost, the pain suffered, the years of internal torment and anguish. What was done cannot be undone. But we can end the silence. We can stop turning our heads away. We can look at you in the eye and finally say on behalf of the American people, what the United States government did was shameful, and I am sorry.

The American people are sorry—for the loss, for the years of hurt. You did nothing wrong, but you were grievously wronged. I apologize and I am sorry that this apology has been so long in coming.

To Macon County, to Tuskegee, to the doctors who have been wrongly associated with the events there, you have our apology, as well. To our African American citizens, I am sorry that your federal government orchestrated a study so clearly racist. That can never be allowed to happen again. It is against everything our country stands for and what we must stand against is what it was.

So let us resolve to hold forever in our hearts and minds the memory of a time not long ago in Macon County, Alabama, so that we can always see how adrift we can become when the rights of any citizens are neglected, ignored, and betrayed. And let us resolve here and now to move forward together.

The legacy of the study at Tuskegee has reached far and deep, in ways that hurt our progress and divide our nation. We cannot be one America when a whole segment of our nation has no trust in America. An apology is the first step, and we take it with a commitment to rebuild that broken thrust. We can begin by making sure there is never again another episode like this one. We need to do more to ensure that medical research practices are sound and ethical, and that researchers work more closely with communities.

Today I would like to announce several steps to help us achieve these goals. First, we will help to build that lasting memorial at Tuskegee. The school founded by Booker T. Washington, distinguished by the renowned scientist George Washington Carver and so many others who advanced the health and well-being of African Americans and all Americans, is a fitting site. The Department of Health and Human Services will award a planning grant so the school can pursue establishing a center for bioethics in research and health care. The center will serve as a museum of the study and support efforts to address its legacy and strengthen bioethics training.

Second, we commit to increase our community involvement so that we may begin restoring lost trust. The study at Tuskegee served to sow distrust of our medical institutions, especially where research is involved. Since the study was halted, abuses have been checked by making informed consent and local review mandatory in federally-funded and mandated research.

Still, 25 years later, many medical studies have little African American participation and African American organ donors are few. This impedes efforts to conduct promising research and to provide the best health care to all our people, including African Americans. So today, I'm directing the Secretary of Health and Human Services, Donna Shalala, to issue a report in 180 days about how we can best involve communities, especially minority communities, in research and health care. You must—every American group must be involved in medical research in ways that are positive. We have put the worst behind us; now we must bring the benefits to all Americans.

Third, we commit to strengthen researchers' training in bioethics. We are constantly working on making breakthroughs in protecting the health of our people and in vanquishing diseases. But all our people must be assured that their rights and dignity will be respected as new drugs, treatments, and therapies are tested and used. So I am directing Secretary Shalala to work in partnership with higher education to prepare training materials for medical researchers. They will be available in a year. They will help researcher build on core ethical principles of respect for individuals, justice and informed consent, and advise them on how to use these principles effectively in diverse populations.

Fourth, to increase and broaden our understanding of ethical issues and clinical research, we commit to providing postgraduate fellowships to train bioethicists, especially among African Americans and other minority groups. HHS will offer these fellowships beginning in September of 1998 to promising students enrolled in bioethics graduate programs.

And, finally, by executive order I am also today extending the charter of the National Bioethics Advisory Commission to October of 1999. The need for this commission is clear. We must be able to call on the thoughtful, collective wisdom of experts and community representatives to find ways to further strengthen our protections for subjects in human research.

We face a challenge in our time. Science and technology are rapidly changing our lives with the promise of making us much healthier, much more productive, and more prosperous. But with these changes we must work harder to see that as we advance we don't leave behind our conscience. No ground is gained and, indeed, much is lost if we lose our moral bearings in the name of progress.

The people who ran the study at Tuskegee diminished the stature of man by abandoning the most basic ethical precepts. They forgot their pledge to heal and repair. They had the power to heal the survivors and all the others and they did not. Today, all we can do is apologize. But you have the power, for only you—Mr.

Shaw, the others who are here, the family members who are with us in tuskegee—only you have the power to forgive. Your presence here shows us that you have chosen a better path than your government did so long ago. You have not withheld the power to forgive. I hope today and tomorrow every American will remember your lesson and live by it.

Thank you and God bless you.

Fred D. Gray, May 16, 1997
Statement at Post-Apology Press Conference

Mr. Howard, Mr. Pollard, Mr. Shaw, Mr. Simmons:

Thank you for your personal efforts to travel from Tuskegee, Alabama, to the White House today. Notwithstanding age, physical infirmities or maladies, you did what was asked of you. This invitation, unlike the one of over 50 years ago, is legitimate, healthy, healing and for the good of many—an apology from the President of the United States for the federal government conducted Tuskegee Syphilis Study. The apology today is seen as a 'beginning' of the healing of emotional wounds and a legacy of suffering, shame, and mistrust on the part of more than 600 Study participants, their heirs and descendants. I hope that it is received in the spirit that I think it is given.

Mr. President, I extend my personal appreciation to you, and the appreciation of all those who are not here today. There are many, touched directly or indirectly by the Tuskegee experiment, who will think well of your gesture here today. And for those who may think this gesture is "too little too late," I hope they will allow it to further validate the worthwhile contribution of all the men who, in many instances, gave their lives. History is the true recorder. Thank you, President Clinton.

To move beyond this "beginning," and to help ensure that the injustices that occurred in the past will not happen again, survivor Herman Shaw said, "When you ride along the highway, you see signs telling you to stop to see certain things. When you think about all the suffering we had for 40 years, a permanent monument is important, so the generations that follow us can stop and read about what happened and realize the things we went through." In this regard, I announce the recent incorporation of the Tuskegee Human and Civil Rights Multicultural Center, a non-profit, tax exempt organization, incorporated in Macon County, Alabama, to establish, develop, promote, and maintain a perpetual and permanent legacy of the significant contributions which these men and others have made in the area of human and civil rights. When fully developed, the Center will recognize the contributions made to the City of Tuskegee, Macon County, the State of Alabama, and the nation. The Center will particularly emphasize the contributions of native Americans, Caucasians or European Americans, and Americans of African descent. Native Americans have a deep and expanded presence in the Tuskegee, Macon County, East Alabama territory.

Tuskegee, Macon County, and East Alabama have a rich heritage. It is full of history. The Tuskegee community and Tuskegee University have jointly played major roles in developing this area. The formation and implementation of such a Center in the city will acknowledge the contribution of both the community and the University. Notwithstanding all of the history that has occurred in Macon County, nothing exists that highlights directly the contribution of all of these groups, including African Americans. When fully developed, it would also mean a substantial economic benefit to the community in tourists dollars.

This is a very ambitious project and will cost millions of dollars to fully develop. When the residents of the city of Montgomery started the Montgomery Bus Boycott it was a very ambitious project, but it ended in the beginning of the Civil Rights Movement. History, particularly civil rights history, records many such accomplishments.

In the spirit of healing racial wounds of division, the Tuskegee Human and Civil Rights Multicultural Center is calling for the support of the federal government, the state, foundations, corporations, organizations, and individuals to financially support the construction of The Center as a permanent legacy of significant achievements in the areas of human and civil rights. We are particularly calling upon the federal government for technical assistance in planning such a permanent legacy.

On behalf of the living participants, the heirs and descendants of participants, this apology is humbly accepted.

Thank you, Mr. President.

Fred Gray Letter to Clinton, May 21, 1997

May 21, 1997

Dear President Clinton:

As counsel for the participants who attended the White House ceremony, the Tuskegee ceremony, Mr. George Key who was unable to attend, and the heirs of deceased participants in the Study, we want to express our genuine appreciation for your invitation to the White House, and the apology made in the East Room on Friday, May 16, 1997. Your consoling words and forthright candor with reference to the Study and the sincere way you spoke and apologized will remain forever in our hearts. You are truly a President who cares for all of the citizens of the nation. On their behalf, we humbly and respectfully accept the apology, and forgive the government for its misconduct.

As Mr. Herman Shaw stated in his remarks, ". . . we want to construct in Tuskegee a PERMANENT MEMORIAL, a place where our children and grandchildren will be able to see the contributions that we, and others, made to this country. I am glad that I have helped form the Tuskegee Human and Civil Rights Multicultural Center, which will be for the purpose of creating such a lasting memorial." Mr. Shaw was referring to the Tuskegee Human and Civil Rights Multicultural Center of which he is a member of the initial board of directors. The Center is a non-profit, tax exempt organization incorporated in Macon County, Alabama, to establish, develop, promote, and maintain the Center as an educational, cultural, and research center, a depository of historic material, exhibition of information with reference to the various ethnic or racial groups who have made contributions to the City of Tuskegee, Alabama, Macon County, Alabama, the State of Alabama, and the United States of America, particularly the contributions of original Native Americans, Caucasians or European Americans, and Americans of African descent.

When fully developed, the Center will not only recognize the contributions made by individuals, including the participants in the Study, but it will assist in bringing the races (red, white, and black) closer together. In addition, it will also result in substantial economic benefit to the City of Tuskegee and Macon County. The participants and family members who attended the ceremony at the White House ratified and confirmed the creation of, and the objects and purposes of the Center. They requested that I solicit your assistance in fully developing the Center.

The first step towards developing such a memorial is appropriate planning. We are requesting your assistance and the assistance of the appropriate governmental agencies to help with technical assistance including planning grants for the Center.

We will always remember what you said and did on Friday, May 16, 1997
Very truly yours,
Fred D. Gray
cc: Mr. Ben Johnson
All participants
Family Members in Attendance at White House Ceremony

Bibliography

Beecher, John. *Collected Poems, 1924–1974.* New York: MacMillan, 1974.

Jones, James H. *Bad Blood: The Tuskegee Syphilis Experiment.* New York: The Free Press, 1981.

Gray, Fred D. *Bus Ride To Justice.* Montgomery: Black Belt Press, 1995.

Gray, Langford, Sapp, McGowan, Gray & Nathanson case files, 1972–1998.

Public Health Service Files and Documents, National Archives.

Mitchell, H. L. *Mean Things Happening in This Land: The Life and Times of H. L. Mitchell, Cofounder of the Southern Tenant Farmers Union.* Allanheld, Osmun & Co., 1979.

Norrell, Robert J. *Reaping The Whirlwind: The Civil Rights Movement in Tuskegee.* New York: Alfred A. Knopf, 1985.

Rosengarten, Theodore. *All God's Dangers: The Life of Nate Shaw.* New York: Alfred A. Knopf, 1974.

Index

About the Author

Fred D. Gray is one of the nation's leading civil rights attorneys. At age 24, he was the lawyer for Rosa Parks, Martin Luther King, Jr., and the Montgomery Bus Boycott, which began the modern Civil Rights Movement. His other cases and clients include the Freedom Riders, the Selma-to-Montgomery March, numerous school desegregation and voting rights lawsuits, and many others.